D1823925

BLACKSTONE'S POLICE

ROAD TRAFFIC

BLACKSTONE'S POLICE

Q & A √

ROAD TRAFFIC

First Edition

Huw Smart and
John Watson

Consultant Editor:
Fraser Sampson

OXFORD
UNIVERSITY PRESS

OXFORD

UNIVERSITY PRESS

Great Clarendon Street, Oxford OX2 6DP

Oxford University Press is a department of the University of Oxford.
It furthers the University's objective of excellence in research, scholarship,
and education by publishing worldwide in

Oxford NewYork

Athens Auckland Bangkok Bogotá Buenos Aires Cape Town
Chennai Dar es Salaam Delhi Florence Hong Kong Istanbul Karachi
Kolkata Kuala Lumpur Madrid Melbourne Mexico City Mumbai Nairobi
Paris São Paulo Shanghai Singapore Taipei Tokyo Toronto Warsaw

with associated companies in Berlin Ibadan

Oxford is a registered trade mark of Oxford University Press
in the UK and certain other countries

Published in the United States
by Oxford University Press Inc., New York

A Blackstone Press Book

© Huw Smart and John Watson 2002

The moral rights of the author have been asserted
Database right Oxford University Press (maker)

All rights reserved. No part of this publication may be reproduced,
stored in a retrieval system, or transmitted, in any form or by any means,
without the prior permission in writing of Oxford University Press,
or as expressly permitted by law, or under terms agreed with the appropriate
reprographics rights organization. Enquiries concerning reproduction
outside the scope of the above should be sent to the Rights Department,
Oxford University Press, at the address above

You must not circulate this book in any other binding or cover
and you must impose the same condition on any acquirer

British Library Cataloguing in Publication Data

Data available

Library of Congress Cataloging in Publication Data

Data available

ISBN 1-84174-303-8

1 3 5 7 9 10 8 6 4 2

Typeset by Style Photosetting Limited, Mayfield, East Sussex
Printed in Great Britain
on acid-free paper by
Ashford Colour Press Limited, Gosport, Hampshire

CONTENTS

Introduction   vii

Acknowledgement   ix

1 Classifications and Concepts   1
Study preparation — Questions — Answers

2 Offences involving Standards of Driving   19
Study preparation — Questions — Answers

3 Notices of Intended Prosecution   33
Study preparation — Questions — Answers

4 Accidents   38
Study preparation — Questions — Answers

5 Drink Driving   45
Study preparation — Questions — Answers

6 Insurance   75
Study preparation — Questions — Answers

7 Safety Measures   82
Study preparation — Questions — Answers

8 Other Measures affecting Safety   89
Study preparation — Questions — Answers

9 Construction and Use   102
Study preparation — Questions — Answers

10 Traffic Signs   112
Study preparation — Questions — Answers

11 Driving Licences   117
Study preparation — Questions — Answers

12 Excise and Registration   128
Study preparation — Questions — Answers

13 Goods and Passenger Vehicles   136
Study preparation — Questions — Answers

14 Fixed Penalty System   150
Study preparation — Questions — Answers

15 Pedal Cycles   155
Study preparation — Questions — Answers

16 Forgery and Falsification   160
Study preparation — Questions — Answers

INTRODUCTION

Before you get into the detail of this book, there are two myths about Multiple Choice Questions (MCQs) that we need to get out of the way right at the start:

1. that they are easy to answer
2. that they are easy to write

Take one look at a professionally designed and properly developed exam paper such as those used by the Police Promotion Examinations Board or the National Board of Medical Examiners in the US and the first myth collapses straight away. Contrary to what some people believe, MCQs are not an easy solution for examiners and not a 'multiple-guess' soft option for examinees.

That is not to say that *all* MCQs are taxing, or even testing — in the psychometric sense. If MCQs are to have any real value at all, they need to be carefully designed and follow some agreed basic rules.

And this leads us to myth number 2.

It is widely assumed by many people and educational organisations that anyone with the knowledge of a subject can write MCQs. You need only look at how few MCQ writing courses are offered by training providers in the UK to see just how far this myth is believed. Similarly, you need only to have a go at a few badly designed MCQs to realise that it *is* a myth none the less. Writing bad MCQs is easy; writing good ones is no easier than answering them!

As with many things, the design of MCQs benefits considerably from time, training and experience. Many MCQ writers fall easily and often unwittingly into the trap of making their questions too hard, too easy or too obscure, or completely different from the type of question that you will eventually encounter in your own particular exam. Others seem to use the MCQ as a way to catch people out or to show how smart they, the authors, are (or think they are).

There are several purposes for which MCQs are very useful. The first is in producing a reliable, valid and fair test of knowledge and understanding across a wide range of subject matter. Another is an aid to study, preparation and revision for such examinations and tests. The differences in objective mean that there are slight differences in the rules that the MCQ writers follow. Whereas the design of fully validated MCQs to be used in high stakes examinations which will effectively determine who passes and who fails have very strict guidelines as to construction, content and style, less stringent rules apply to MCQs that are being used for teaching and revision. For that reason, there may be types of MCQ that are appropriate in the latter setting which would not be used in the former. However, in developing the MCQs for this book, the authors have tried to follow the fundamental rules of MCQ design but they would not claim to have replicated the level of psychometric rigour that is — and has to be — adopted by the type of examining bodies referred to above.

These MCQs are designed to reinforce your knowledge and understanding, to highlight any gaps or weaknesses in that knowledge and understanding and to help focus your revision of the relevant topics.

I hope that we have achieved that aim.

Good luck!

ACKNOWLEDGEMENTS

As qualified police trainers, we have written this book to complement *Blackstone's Police Manuals* and to provide a source of improving knowledge of police-related legislation. It is important to recognise that full study of the relevant chapters in the *Police Manuals* is recommended before attempting the Questions and Answers.

Particular attention should be paid to **Answers** section and students should always ask themselves, 'Why did I get the question wrong?' and just as importantly 'Why did I get the question right'. Combining the information gained from self-questioning and the information contained in the **Answers** section should lead to a greater understanding of the subject matter.

We wish to thank Alistair MacQueen for his faith, Heather Saward for pulling it all together and Fraser Sampson for his words of wisdom. Thanks also to Jane Kavanagh at Oxford University Press for her continuing support of the project.

Huw would like to thank Julie for her patience and understanding during long evenings and weekends of work, Ian, Debbie, Theresa and Vince at Detail Technologies Limited for all their hard work.

John would like to thank Sue for her patience and understanding during long evenings and weekends of work and remind David, Catherine and Andrew that Daddy is not just the man who sits in the corner working on his computer.

1 CLASSIFICATIONS AND CONCEPTS

STUDY PREPARATION

The classifications and concepts set out in road traffic legislation are critical to understanding and proving many — if not all — the relevant offences. There is little point in knowing that a particular offence can only be committed by a motor vehicle for instance, if you don't recognise a 'motor vehicle' when you come across one.

The classifications and concepts addressed in this chapter are therefore the building blocks for the rest of the subjects that follow — so they are well worth careful study.

QUESTIONS

Question 1

ARMSTRONG owns a vintage car, which he takes to shows, by loading it onto a trailer and towing it. The vintage car was manufactured in 1939, and was used on the road until 1970. ARMSTRONG, however, has never used the car on the road since he bought it.

Would ARMSTRONG's car be a motor vehicle in these circumstances?

[A] No, as the vehicle is not currently being used on the road.
[B] Yes, but only if ARMSTRONG intends to use the vehicle on the road in future.
[C] Yes, regardless of ARMSTRONG's intent as to the future use of the vehicle.
[D] No, as ARMSTRONG has not adapted the vehicle for use on roads.

Question 2

NEWBERRY removed the engine from his car, and arranged for his friend, SIMMONDS to help him tow the car to a garage to have a new engine fitted. They were stopped by the police while towing the car on a road.

In relation to the status of the vehicle when it was stopped, which of the following statements is correct?

[A] It was both mechanically propelled and a motor vehicle.
[B] It was still mechanically propelled, but was not a motor vehicle.
[C] It was still a motor vehicle, but was not mechanically propelled.
[D] It was neither a motor vehicle nor mechanically propelled.

Question 3

In relation to the definition of a 'passenger vehicle', which of the following statements, if either, is correct?

1. If a vehicle has been adapted to carry passengers and their effects, as well as goods, it will still be a 'passenger vehicle'.
2. If a passenger vehicle is constructed to carry more than 8 but fewer than 16 passengers, it will be classed as a 'mini-bus'.

[A] Statement 1 only.
[B] Statement 2 only.
[C] Both statements.
[D] Neither statement.

Question 4

In respect of the definition of a 'medium-sized goods vehicle' (including its permissible weight and the number of passengers it may carry), which of the following statements is correct?

[A] More than 3 tonnes, no more than 9 passengers including the driver.
[B] More than 3.5 tonnes, no more than 9 passengers excluding the driver.
[C] More than 3.5 tonnes, no limit on the number of passengers.
[D] More than 3.5 tonnes, no more than 9 passengers including the driver.

Question 5

Section 108(1) of the Road Traffic Act 1988 defines a 'moped'. In respect of a 'moped' first used after the 1 August 1977, which of the following statements is correct?

[A] It must have an engine size that does not exceed 125 cc and a maximum speed of 50 mph.
[B] It must have an engine size that does not exceed 50 cc and be fitted with pedals.
[C] It must have an engine size that does not exceed 50 cc and a maximum speed of 50 mph.
[D] It must have an engine size that does not exceed 50 cc and be propelled by electric power.

Question 6

In relation to the term 'accident', which of the following statements, if either, is/are true?

1. When determining whether or not an accident has occurred, the court will apply the test of what an ordinary person would think.
2. The term 'accident' will not include a deliberate act committed by the driver of a vehicle.

[A] Statement 1 only.
[B] Statement 2 only.
[C] Both statements.
[D] Neither statement.

Question 7

CLIFFORD was driving his car and his wife LISA was in the front passenger seat. CLIFFORD's mobile phone rang, but it had fallen behind his seat. CLIFFORD asked LISA to steer the car while he reached for his phone. LISA took hold of the wheel, but the car veered across the carriageway and collided with a lamp post, causing substantial damage to it.

Who may be charged in relation to 'driving' in these circumstances?

[A] LISA is not liable, as only one person may be the driver of a vehicle at any one time.
[B] LISA and CLIFFORD could both be held to be the driver of the vehicle.
[C] LISA and CLIFFORD could both be held to be the driver of the vehicle, provided they are not charged with dangerous driving.
[D] Either LISA or CLIFFORD could be held to be the driver, but to charge both is not permitted in relation to road traffic offences.

Question 8

In which of the following scenarios will the person probably **not** be deemed to be 'driving' a vehicle?

1. McDONAGH was pushing his car, while leaning through the window to steer it.
2. GUNNEL was sitting astride his motorbike and was pushing it along with both feet.
3. JONES was the front seat passenger in a car and grabbed the steering wheel suddenly to stop the driver hitting a cat.

[A] All three scenarios.
[B] None of the above scenarios.
[C] Scenarios 1 and 3 only.
[D] Scenario 2 only.

Question 9

KELLY was drunk and decided to drive home. KELLY opened his car door and sat in the driver's seat. However, when he tried to start the car, KELLY could not do so because he was using his house keys. Eventually KELLY managed to find the correct key, but the car would not start, as the battery was flat.

In these circumstances, which would be the first point at which KELLY has 'attempted' to drive his car?

[A] He did not attempt to drive the car at any time.
[B] When he tried to start the car with the correct key.
[C] When he first sat in the driver's seat.
[D] When he tried to start the car with the house key.

Question 10

WATKINS borrowed his friend's car one evening and went out drinking. On his way home, he went to a takeaway restaurant. WATKINS was overheard by CARTER, boasting about driving home. It was obvious that WATKINS was drunk and CARTER telephoned the police. WATKINS was leaving the premises when the police arrived.

In relation to the proof required to establish whether a person is 'in charge' of a vehicle, which of the following is true?

[A]   WATKINS must show that there was no likelihood of him resuming control of the vehicle while he was drunk.
[B]   The prosecution must show that WATKINS intended to drive the vehicle in the future.
[C]   WATKINS must show that he had no intention of resuming control of the vehicle while he was drunk.
[D]   The prosecution must show that there was a likelihood of WATKINS driving the vehicle in the future.

Question 11

HILTON took his car to MOHAMMED's garage for repairs. About five minutes after HILTON left, MOHAMMED had to park the car in the road to make room for another car. As MOHAMMED was walking away from the car, Constable DAVIES was walking past and noticed that it was not displaying a vehicle excise licence.

Who would be the 'keeper' of the vehicle in these circumstances?

[A]   HILTON only, as he is the owner of the vehicle.
[B]   MOHAMMED only.
[C]   Neither, as the vehicle was not on the road for long.
[D]   Both MOHAMMED and HILTON.

Question 12

HAWKINS was involved in a road traffic accident. HAWKINS was to blame, having travelled through a red traffic light. When the police arrived, HAWKINS told the officer that she was diabetic and had blacked out momentarily, having suffered a hypoglycaemic episode.

Would HAWKINS be able to rely on this as a defence in these circumstances?

[A] No, HAWKINS has no defence in these circumstances.
[B] Yes, such an attack would provide an automatic defence.
[C] Yes, provided she could show the attack was unforeseen.
[D] No, even though the element of *mens rea* is not present, the *actus reus* is.

Question 13

In which of the following scenarios, if either, will the vehicle be 'on a road' as defined by s. 192(1) of the Road Traffic Act 1988?

1. RANDALL parked his van on his driveway; however, the rear of the vehicle was sticking out and blocking the pavement.
2. LANG was seen riding a motorcycle without a helmet, on a public bridleway.

[A] Scenario 1 only.
[B] Scenario 2 only.
[C] Both scenarios.
[D] Neither scenario.

Question 14

VIVIER arranged a Scout fête, and was given permission to use a field belonging to GILES, a local farmer. On the day of the fête, entry was restricted to members of the local Scout groups, and drivers of vehicles were charged £1 each for entry.

In relation to road traffic offences, would GILES' field qualify as a 'public' place in these circumstances?

[A] No, as entry to the field was restricted to certain people.
[B] Yes, as members of the public were allowed access.
[C] Yes, people were using the field with GILES' permission.
[D] No, as the people using the field were charged for entry.

Question 15

In relation to the term 'public place', which of the following statements, if either, is/are correct?

1. It will be for the defence to prove that a place is not a 'public place', in cases where a dispute arises.
2. For a public place to be converted into a private place, a physical obstruction must be in place to prevent general entry.

[A] Statement 1 only.
[B] Statement 2 only.
[C] Both statements.
[D] Neither statement.

Question 16

BAKER was driving a tractor and towing a trailer laden with hay on a road, on behalf of his employer, RICHARDSON. Constable SHAH stopped BAKER for having an insecure load, as some of the bales fell off the trailer onto the road. Constable SHAH reported BAKER for the offence and later spoke to RICHARDSON, who denied responsibility as BAKER had loaded the trailer himself. RICHARDSON stated he would not have authorised the load to be carried in such a manner.

Would RICHARDSON be guilty of 'using' a vehicle in these circumstances?

[A] No, as he did not authorise BAKER to use the vehicle in such a way.
[B] No, as BAKER was not acting in the course of his employment.
[C] No, as BAKER was drawing a trailer, only he could 'use' it.
[D] Yes, he would be guilty in these circumstances alone.

Question 17

In relation to the term 'using' a vehicle, which of the following statements, if either, is/are correct?

1. If a vehicle is on a road and is in an unroadworthy condition, the owner cannot be said to be using it.
2. The passenger in a vehicle cannot be guilty of using it in any circumstances.

[A] Statement 1 only.
[B] Statement 2 only.
[C] Both statements.
[D] Neither statement.

Question 18

PRICE is the transport manager of a haulage company. He knows that most of his drivers make false entries on their tachograph sheets. PRICE has not instructed them to do this, but as it means that the drivers work longer hours on behalf of the company, he does not stop them. HILLMAN, the owner of the company, is unaware of what is happening.

Are either PRICE or HILLMAN guilty of 'causing' offences in relation to drivers' hours in these circumstances?

[A] Yes, PRICE only, as he has turned a blind eye to what is happening.
[B] No, neither person is guilty of 'causing' offences in these circumstances.
[C] Yes, HILLMAN only as the owner of the company.
[D] Yes, both people would be 'causing' offences in these circumstances.

Question 19

Generally, in order to prove an offence of 'permitting', it will be necessary to show some knowledge by the defendant of the use of his or her vehicle.

What must you prove the defendant knew in order for him or her to be guilty of 'permitting'?

[A] Knowledge only that the vehicle was being used on a road.
[B] Knowledge by the defendant of the vehicle's use or of the unlawful nature of that use.
[C] Knowledge only by the defendant of the vehicle's use.
[D] Knowledge by the defendant of the vehicle's use and of the unlawful nature of that use.

ANSWERS

Question 1

Answer **C** — A motor vehicle is a mechanically propelled vehicle, intended *or* adapted for use on roads. It follows that if a vehicle is not intended or adapted for use on roads, it will not be a motor vehicle for these purposes.

A vehicle is 'intended' for use on the roads, if it was intended that it should be so used *when it was manufactured.* It is immaterial that it is not being used on a road now and answer A is therefore incorrect.

The test will be an objective one — but it does *not* look at the intention of the owner (*Chief Constable of Avon and Somerset* v *F (A Juvenile)* [1987] RTR 378). Answer B is therefore incorrect.

Answer D is incorrect because it is immaterial whether the vehicle has been adapted for use on roads, as it was intended to be so used.

Question 2

Answer **A** — Removing an engine from a vehicle does not stop it from being 'mechanically propelled', if you can show that the engine can easily be replaced (*Newberry* v *Simmonds* [1961] 2 All ER 318. Answers C and D are therefore incorrect.

A vehicle that is being towed by another will still be a motor vehicle (*Cobb* v *Whorton* [1971] RTR 392. Answers B and D are therefore incorrect.

Question 3

Answer **B** — Statement 1 is incorrect. If a vehicle has been adapted to carry passengers and their effects, as well as goods, it will *not* be a 'passenger vehicle' (*Flower Freight Co. Ltd* v *Hammond* [1963] 1 QB 275).

Statement 2 is a correct statement. A passenger-carrying vehicle, which is constructed to carry more than 8 but fewer than 16 passengers, will be classed as a 'mini-bus'. (If the figure is more than 16, the vehicle will be classed as a 'large bus'.)

Consequently, answers A, C and D are incorrect.

Question 4

Answer **D** — Under s. 108(1) of the Road Traffic Act 1988, 'medium-sized' goods vehicles are those constructed to carry or haul goods, which are not adapted to carry more than nine passengers, *including* the driver.

The maximum permissible weight of such a vehicle will exceed 3.5 tonnes.

Answer D is the only option that covers accurately both points and therefore answers A, B and C are incorrect.

Question 5

Answer **C** — Under s. 108(1) of the Road Traffic Act 1988, the definition of a 'moped' is divided between those that were first used before 1 August 1977, and those first used on or after this date. Early mopeds (i.e. those in the first group) had to have pedals fitted, with an engine size not exceeding 50 cc. There was no restriction on speed. Answer B is therefore incorrect because pedals were not required on mopeds first used after the relevant date.

Mopeds which fall into the newer category are required to have a maximum design speed of 50 mph and an engine size not exceeding 50 cc.

Answers A and D are a mixture of the definition of a moped, and the definition of a 'Learner Motor Bicycle' (which must *either* be propelled by electric power *or* have an engine size not exceeding 125cc) and are therefore incorrect.

Question 6

Answer **A** — Statement 1 is a correct statement. The court will, when determining whether or not an accident has occurred, apply the test of what an ordinary person would think.

Statement 2 is an incorrect statement. The term 'accident' *will* include a deliberate act committed by the driver of a vehicle, such as ramming a gate (*Chief Constable of Staffordshire* v *Lees* [1981] RTR 506).

Consequently, answers B, C and D are incorrect.

Question 7

Answer **B** — It is possible for more than one person to be the 'driver' of a vehicle as s. 192(1) of the Road Traffic Act 1988 makes provision for the 'steersman' to be a 'driver'. This was confirmed in the case of *Tyler* v *Whatmore* [1976] RTR 83, when one person was sitting in the driver's seat and the other leaned across and operated the steering wheel. Answer A is therefore incorrect.

The only situation where the above rule does not apply is in a case of causing death by dangerous driving under s. 1 of the 1988 Act. Answer C is incorrect, as the rule *will* apply in the case of dangerous driving.

Answer D is incorrect because the rule does allow for both to be charged, subject to the exception above.

Question 8

Answer **C** — The question is designed to test whether a person is **not** driving a vehicle. There are many different cases ruling on whether or not a person is 'driving' a vehicle. This is because the question is one of *fact* and courts are largely left to decide each on its own merits.

The three cases covered by the question offer helpful guidance. In *R* v *MacDonagh* [1974] RTR 372, the defendant was pushing his car, while leaning through the window to steer it. He was held *not* to be 'driving'. The person *was* 'driving' in *Gunnel* v *DPP* [1993] RTR 619, where the person was sitting astride his motorbike and was pushing it along with both feet. In *Jones* v *Pratt* [1983] RTR 54, the person was *not* driving when he was the front seat passenger in a car and grabbed the steering wheel suddenly, to stop the driver hitting an animal.

Contrast *Jones* v *Pratt* with *Tyler* v *Whatmore* in question 7. The main difference between the two cases would appear to be that in the latter case, Tyler was in control for a little while, whereas in the former, Jones was in control only momentarily. However, as this is a question of fact, there are no guarantees that a court will follow these approaches in every case.

Consequently, answers A, B and D are incorrect.

Question 9

Answer **D** — Acts which are merely preparatory will not amount to attempting to drive. Merely sitting in a car would not be sufficient, as this is still a preparatory act. Answer C is therefore incorrect.

It has been held that, where a defendant sits in the driver's seat of a car and tries to put their house keys in the ignition, that behaviour may be enough to prove a charge of 'attempting to drive' (*Kelly* v *Hogan* [1982] RTR 352). Answer A is therefore incorrect.

The fact that the vehicle is incapable of being driven will not prevent a charge involving an 'attempt' to drive (*R* v *Farrance* [1978] RTR 225). Answer B is incorrect because the question asks for the *first* point at which the defendant could be guilty of 'attempting' to drive.

Question 10

Answer **A** — The case of *DPP* v *Watkins* [1989] 2 WLR 966 outlines the principles to be applied when considering whether or not a person is 'in charge' of a vehicle.

Where the defendant is the owner of the vehicle *or* where he has recently driven it, it will be for him to show that there was no likelihood of his resuming control while he was drunk.

Where the defendant is not the owner or has not recently driven the vehicle, the prosecution will only need to show that the defendant was in voluntary control of the vehicle or intended to become so in the immediate future. Answers B and D are incorrect for this reason.

Answer C is incorrect, as the defendant must show that it is *unlikely* that he will drive while unfit, not that he had no *intention* of doing so — a slight difference in wording, but nevertheless important in the context of the case.

Question 11

Answer **B** — The 'keeper' of a vehicle can be a different person to the 'owner'. Whereas the 'owner' of the vehicle will remain so until they dispose of the vehicle, the 'keeper' can cease to be so if they temporarily part with the vehicle (*R* v *Parking Adjudicator, ex parte The Mayor and Burgesses of the London Borough Council of Wandsworth*, 10 July 1996, unreported).

Therefore, while Hilton has not transferred ownership of the vehicle, he is no longer the 'keeper', albeit on a temporary basis. Answers A and D are therefore incorrect.

Section 62(2) of the Vehicle Excise and Registration Act 1994 states that a person 'keeps' the vehicle if he or she causes it to be on a road for any period, however short, when it is not in use there. Therefore, answer C is incorrect.

Question 12

Answer **C** — When a person's movements are beyond their control, or their actions are involuntary, they will not generally be liable in criminal law as the element of *actus reus* is not present. It is also highly likely that because there is no willed action or omission by the defendant, he or she will not have the required state of mind (*mens rea*). A defence is provided in such circumstances, namely 'automatism'. Answers A and D are therefore incorrect.

There is no automatic defence of *automatism*; it will only be available in certain circumstances (answer B is therefore incorrect). If a person has a particular medical condition, which is likely to occur when they are driving, they have a duty to take reasonable steps to avoid driving when the symptoms are likely to arise (*R* v *Sibbles* [1959] Crim LR 660). This case is supported by the case of *Moss* v *Winder* [1981] RTR 37 (which relates specifically to a diabetic undergoing a hypoglycaemic attack).

Question 13

Answer **C** — The vehicle will be 'on a road' in both scenarios. In relation to scenario 1, if a vehicle is partly on the road and partly on some other privately-owned land, it can be treated as being on a 'road' for the purposes of road traffic legislation (*Randall* v *Motor Insurers' Bureau* [1969] 1 All ER 21).

The answer to scenario 2 is slightly more complicated. The definition of a road, under s. 192(1) of the Road Traffic Act 1988 includes, 'any highway'. A 'highway' is a way over which the public has a right to pass and re-pass by foot, horse or vehicle (*Lang* v *Hindhaugh* [1986] RTR 271). Highways will include 'public bridleways'. Therefore, logically, if a 'bridleway' is a 'highway', and a 'highway' is a 'road', then a 'bridleway' is also a 'road'.

Consequently, answers A, B and D are incorrect.

Question 14

Answer **A** — In order for a place to be a 'public place', it must be shown by the prosecution that:

- the people admitted to the place are members of the public and are admitted for that reason, and not because they belong to a certain or special class of the public, *and*
- those people are so admitted with the permission, express or implied, of the owner of the land.

(*DPP* v *Vivier* [1991] RTR 205).

The above case shows that the place in question must be open to *all* members of the public, without restriction (answer B is therefore incorrect). It is irrelevant whether the people are there with permission if only restricted members of the public are present. The two requirements from the *Vivier* case go hand in hand and answer C is therefore incorrect.

The fact that people had to pay to enter the land is completely irrelevant as to whether it is a public place. It is the *class of people* that are allowed entry (or not) that is important. If the fête had been open to *all* members of the public and they had all been made to pay, it would have been a public place. (Answer D is therefore incorrect).

Question 15

Answer **B** — Statement 1 is incorrect. In cases where a dispute arises as to whether a place is a 'public place', it will be for the *prosecution* to show that it is in fact a public place.

Statement 2 is a correct statement. For a place which is ostensibly *public* in its nature to become a *private* place either permanently or temporarily, there needs to be some form of physical obstruction to overcome in order to enter that place (*R* v *Waters* (1963) 107 SJ 275).

Consequently, answers A, C and D are incorrect.

Question 16

Answer **D** — Offences relating to 'using' a vehicle are generally committed by the driver and the driver's employer. For the employer to commit the offence of 'using', the person driving the vehicle must be doing so in the ordinary course of his employer's business (*West Yorkshire Trading Standards Service* v *Lex Vehicle Leasing Ltd* [1996] RTR 170). It must be proved that:

- the employer owned the vehicle,
- the driver was employed by the employer, and
- the driver was driving in the ordinary course of his employment

(*Jones* v *DPP* [1999] RTR 1).

It is immaterial that the employer has not specifically authorised the employee to use the vehicle in such a way (*Richardson* v *Baker* [1976] RTR 56). Answers A and B are therefore incorrect.

The owner of a trailer who is responsible for putting it on a road will not escape liability by arguing that it was being drawn and therefore 'used' by someone else (*N.F.C. Forwarding Ltd* v *DPP* [1989] RTR 239). Answer C is therefore incorrect.

Question 17

Answer **D** — Statement 1 is incorrect. If a vehicle is shown to be a 'motor vehicle' and it is on a road, it may be said to be in 'use', even if it is in such a state that it cannot be driven (*Pumbien* v *Vines* [1996] RTR 37.

Statement 2 is also incorrect. It is generally the case that a passenger in a car does not 'use' the vehicle. However, if a passenger arranges to travel in or on a vehicle for his or her benefit, he or she will 'use' the vehicle (*Cobb* v *Williams* [1973] RTR 113). A passenger can also 'use' a vehicle if there is an element of 'joint enterprise' (*O'Mahoney* v *Jollife* [1999] RTR 245).

Consequently, answers A, B and C are incorrect.

Question 18

Answer **B** — 'Causing' will involve some degree of dominance or control, or express mandate from the 'causer'.

Causing requires both positive action and knowledge by the defendant, (*Price* v *Cromack* [1975] 1 WLR 988). Therefore it is not enough that the person in charge is aware an offence is being committed; he or she must have done something to contribute to it. Neither person in the scenario could meet these criteria, as neither 'ordered' the offences to be committed (one person was unaware of what was going on).

Further, wilful blindness by employers to their employees' unlawful actions is not enough to amount to 'causing' the offence. Answers A, C and D are incorrect for these reasons.

Question 19

Answer **D** — Generally in order to prove a case of 'permitting' there must be proof of knowledge by the defendant of the vehicle's use *and* of the unlawful nature of that use. In other words, there must be proof that the defendant knew the vehicle was being used and that the driver was committing an offence by using it. Answers A, B and C are incorrect for this reason.

2 OFFENCES INVOLVING STANDARDS OF DRIVING

STUDY PREPARATION

Offences involving standards of driving are among the most frequently encountered of road traffic offences. The key to understanding such offences — and any relevant defences — lies in knowing:

- the classification of vehicle covered by the offence
- the *place* in which the offence can be committed
- the mental element required

It should be noted that there is only one standard of driving that is acceptable of any driver, irrespective of his or her particular driving experience or qualifications.

It is also worth noting the application of road traffic law to police drivers and those from other emergency services.

QUESTIONS

Question 1

Which statement below most accurately describes where an offence may be committed, and in which type of vehicle, under s. 1 of the Road Traffic Act 1988 (causing death by dangerous driving)?

[A]   Motor vehicle, on a road only.
[B]   Mechanically propelled vehicle, on a road or public place.
[C]   Motor vehicle, on a road or public place.
[D]   Mechanically propelled vehicle, on a road only.

Question 2

HENNIGAN was driving a stolen vehicle and WEBB was a passenger. They were driving at 60 mph, approaching a junction, when HENNIGAN told WEBB to pull the handbrake up. He tried to do a handbrake turn, but lost control when WEBB pulled the handbrake, and collided with a wall. WEBB was killed in the accident, but HENNIGAN survived.

Would HENNIGAN be guilty of causing the death of WEBB by dangerous driving in these circumstances?

[A]   Yes, if it can be shown he was a substantial cause of WEBB's death.
[B]   No, as WEBB contributed substantially to his own death.
[C]   Yes, if it can be shown he was the sole cause of WEBB's death.
[D]   Yes, if it can be shown he contributed in some way to WEBB's death.

Question 3

DALEY was driving her car on the approach to a zebra crossing when some children were crossing the road. When DALEY applied her brakes, they failed and she knocked over a child, injuring her. DALEY's car was examined and it was found that her brake discs were worn so much that they did not work. DALEY stated that she had heard the brakes squealing earlier in her journey, but had not realised how bad they were.

What further evidence, if any, would be required in order to convict DALEY of driving dangerously?

[A] That it would have been obvious to a competent and careful driver that driving the vehicle in that condition would be dangerous.

[B] No further evidence is required; DALEY may be convicted on these facts alone.

[C] DALEY could not be convicted of dangerous driving, as she was unaware of the dangerous condition of her car.

[D] That it should have been obvious to DALEY that driving the vehicle in that condition would be dangerous.

Question 4

NEWMAN was involved in an accident, where he drove into the wall of a house, situated on a sharp bend. Nobody was injured in the accident, but substantial damage was caused to the house. There were no witnesses to the accident itself, however, GORDON told the police that NEWMAN had overtaken her before the bend, and in her opinion, he was driving too fast.

What evidence would GORDON be able to give, in order to support a prosecution against NEWMAN for dangerous driving?

[A] None, as no people suffered injury or death as a direct result of the accident.

[B] That the vehicle was driven below the standards expected of a competent and careful driver, prior to the accident.

[C] None, as GORDON was not a witness to the accident itself, her evidence amounts to 'hearsay' evidence.

[D] That the vehicle was driven far below the standards expected of a competent and careful driver, prior to the accident.

Question 5

Which of the following statements, if either, is/are correct in relation to offences under ss. 1 and 2A of the Road Traffic Act 1988 (causing death by dangerous driving and dangerous driving)?

1. A person convicted of an offence under s. 1 may also be guilty of manslaughter.
2. A person may be convicted of dangerous driving if the load they are carrying on their vehicle is considered to be 'dangerous'.

[A] Statement 1 only.
[B] Statement 2 only.
[C] Both statements.
[D] Neither statement.

Question 6

McCRONE was involved in a road traffic accident, when he drove into a parked car, having lost concentration momentarily. At the time of the accident, McCRONE was learning to drive in a driving school car and was accompanied by RIDING, his driving instructor.

In relation to McCRONE's state of mind, what would the prosecution need to prove in order to convict him of driving without due care and attention?

[A] Either that McCRONE knew, or was aware of the fact that his driving fell far below the required standard.
[B] The prosecution have nothing to prove in relation to McCRONE's state of mind, there is no statutory defence.
[C] That McCRONE was aware of the fact that his driving fell below the required standard.
[D] The prosecution have nothing to prove in relation to McCRONE's state of mind, but he may have a statutory defence due to his inexperience.

Question 7

DILKS was driving his car in the open-air car park of a large shopping centre, on a busy Saturday. It was raining heavily and DILKS decided to soak some pedestrians by driving through puddles. The first group he picked on were standing in a bus shelter. DILKS drove past and sprayed water on the shelter window and nobody got wet. The second group was not protected and several people were soaked as a result of his actions.

Has DILKS committed an offence under s. 3 of the Road Traffic Act 1988, by driving without due consideration?

[A]   Yes, but only in relation to the second group of pedestrians.
[B]   No, as no other drivers were affected by his actions.
[C]   Yes, in relation to both groups of pedestrians.
[D]   No, as the incidents did not take place on a road.

Question 8

Section 3A of the Road Traffic Act 1988 deals with offences of causing death by careless driving while the offending driver is under the influence of drink or drugs, or is over the prescribed limit.

Under s. 3A(1)(c), a police officer may make a request for a sample for analysis from the driver suspected of committing such an offence. When may the request be made?

[A]   Within 18 hours of the accident being reported.
[B]   Within 18 hours of the time of death.
[C]   Within 18 hours of a roadside breath test.
[D]   Within 18 hours of the accident.

Question 9

Which of the following statements, if either, is/are correct in relation to an offence committed under s. 3A of the Road Traffic Act 1988 (causing death by careless driving while under the influence of drink or drugs or over the prescribed limit)?

1. An offence may only be committed under this section by a person driving a motor vehicle.
2. An offence may be committed under this section on a road or a public place.

[A] Statement 1 only.
[B] Statement 2 only.
[C] Both statements.
[D] Neither statement.

Question 10

Section 38(7) of the Road Traffic Act 1988 refers to the use of the Highway Code in court proceedings. In relation to s. 38, which of the following statements, if either, is/are correct?

1. A failure by a person to observe a provision of the Highway Code may be used in civil proceedings only, to establish or negative any liability as to their driving.
2. The braking distances shown in the Highway Code are admissible in proving speeding cases in court.

[A] Statement 1 only.
[B] Statement 2 only.
[C] Both statements.
[D] Neither statement.

Question 11

Constable PIERCE was dealing with a road traffic accident, which involved serious injuries to one driver. The driver of the other vehicle left the scene without stopping. A PNC check revealed that the registered keeper of the vehicle, LOWE, lived nearby. Constable PIERCE attended LOWE's address immediately to ascertain who was driving the vehicle.

What does s. 172 of the Road Traffic Act 1988 say in relation to Constable PIERCE's ability to ascertain these details?

[A] A request may be made verbally by Constable PIERCE, and LOWE has 28 days in which to reply.

[B] A request may only be made by post, and LOWE would have 28 days in which to reply.

[C] A request may be made verbally by Constable PIERCE, and LOWE must reply immediately.

[D] Constable PIERCE may not make the request, this power is restricted to people authorised by the chief officer of police.

Question 12

O'TOOLE was driving an ambulance to a serious injury road traffic accident. O'TOOLE had activated the siren and flashing lights and was approaching a junction controlled by traffic lights, which were showing red. O'TOOLE slowed down on her approach, but drove through the red light. RICHARDS approached in his car from the nearside, and drove through a green light, and collided with the ambulance.

In relation to O'TOOLE's driving, which of the following statements is correct?

[A] Emergency service crews are entitled to pass through red lights, and O'TOOLE may rely on this exemption to defend her driving.

[B] O'TOOLE may be guilty of driving without due care and attention, but may have a defence as she had warned other drivers of her approach.

[C] O'TOOLE may be guilty of driving without due care and attention, but may have a defence because of the serious nature of the accident she was attending.

[D] O'TOOLE will be guilty of driving without due care and attention and she has no defence available to her.

Question 13

MARTIN owed BELL a considerable amount of money. BELL threatened to set fire to MARTIN's car if the money was not paid immediately. MARTIN persuaded his brother to lend him the money and he drove to BELL's house. On his way, MARTIN was stopped by the police, who discovered he was a disqualified driver. MARTIN claimed he was acting under duress, and would not have driven had it not been for the threat made by BELL.

Would MARTIN be entitled to claim a defence of duress in these circumstances?

[A] No, the defence will only apply where death is threatened.
[B] No, the defence will only apply where death or serious injury are threatened.
[C] Yes, the defence will apply where serious damage has been threatened.
[D] No, the defence will not apply in a case of disqualified driving.

ANSWERS

Question 1

Answer **B** — The offence of causing death by dangerous driving under s. 1 of the Road Traffic Act 1988 may be committed by a person driving a mechanically propelled vehicle on a road or public place. The Act gives a wide meaning to the types of vehicle that may commit the offence (including dumper trucks, cranes and quad bikes), and the location. Answers A, C and D are therefore incorrect.

Question 2

Answer **D** — To prove an offence under s. 1 of the Road Traffic Act 1988 (causing death by dangerous driving), it must be shown that a person other than the defendant died. The driving by the defendant must be shown to have been *a* cause of the death. It is not necessary to show that it was the sole or even a substantial cause of death (*R* v *Hennigan* [1971] 3 All ER 133). Answers A and C are therefore incorrect.

It is irrelevant whether or not the person killed contributed to the incident, which resulted in his or her death. Answer B is therefore incorrect.

Question 3

Answer **A** — Section 2A(2) of the Road Traffic Act 1988 states:

(2)   A person is also to be regarded as driving dangerously for the purposes of sections 1 and 2 above if it would be obvious to a competent and careful driver that driving the vehicle in its current state would be dangerous.

The test is an objective one which looks at the manner of driving and *not* at the defendant's state of mind. It must be proved that:

- the dangerous condition would itself have been obvious to a competent and careful driver, *or*
- the defendant actually *knew* of its condition

(*R* v *Strong* [1995] Crim LR 428).

Answer B is incorrect, as the prosecution has to prove one of the above requirements.

Answer C is incorrect for the same reason.

Answer D is incorrect as the dangerous driving must have been obvious to a competent and careful driver — not simply to Daley herself.

Question 4

Answer **D** — For the purposes of s. 1 of the Road Traffic Act 1988, under s. 2A(1) of the Act a person is to be regarded as driving dangerously if:

> (a)   the way he drives falls *far* below what would be expected of a competent and careful driver, and
> (b)   it would be obvious to a competent and careful driver that driving in that way would be dangerous.

(Answer B is incorrect, as the 'far' is missing.)

Answer C is incorrect because evidence showing how a particular vehicle was being driven before the incident itself may be given in support of the charge of dangerous driving. Gordon's 'opinion' would be relevant, because of the wording of s. 2A(1)(b) above.

Under s. 2A(3) of the 1988 Act, 'dangerous' refers to danger either of injury to a person *or* of serious damage to property. Answer A is therefore incorrect.

Question 5

Answer **C** — Both statements are correct. In relation to statement 1, an offence under s. 1 of the Road Traffic Act 1988 *may* also amount to manslaughter (*R* v *Governor of Holloway Prison, ex parte Jennings* [1983] 1 AC 624).

In relation to statement 2, s. 2A(2) of the 1988 Act states that a person will be guilty of dangerous driving if it would be obvious to a competent and careful driver that driving the vehicle in its current state would be dangerous.

Section 2A(4) of the Act goes on to say that in determining for the purposes of subsection (2) the state of the vehicle, regard may be had to anything attached to or carried on it or in it and to the manner in which it is attached or carried.

Consequently, answers A, B and D are incorrect.

Question 6

Answer **B** — 'Due care and attention' is the standard of driving that would be expected from a reasonable, prudent and competent driver in all the attendant circumstances. Once the prosecution has proved that the defendant has departed from that standard, and that his or her actions were 'voluntary', the offence is complete. There is no requirement to prove any *knowledge* or *awareness* by the defendant that his or her driving fell below that standard (*R* v *Lawrence* [1981] RTR 217). Answers A and C are therefore incorrect. There is only one *objective* standard of driving, which is expected of *all* drivers — even learner drivers (*McCrone* v *Riding* [1938] 1 All ER 157). Answer D is therefore incorrect.

Question 7

Answer **A** — An offence is committed under s. 3 of the Road Traffic Act 1988 when a person drives a mechanically propelled vehicle on a road or public place, without due care and attention, or without due consideration for other persons using the road *or place*. As the offence may be committed in a public place, answer D is incorrect.

Other persons using the road/public place can include pedestrians who are deliberately sprayed with water from a puddle or passengers in a vehicle (*Pawley* v *Wharldall* [1965] 2 All ER 757. Answer B is therefore incorrect.

It must be shown that some other person was inconvenienced by the defendant's actions (*Dilks* v *Bowman Shaw* [1981] RTR 4). No people were affected in the first group, answer C is therefore incorrect.

Question 8

Answer **D** — Under s. 3A(1)(c) of the Road Traffic Act 1988, a police officer may request a sample from the driver who has committed an offence under s. 3A(1), within 18 hours of the *driving which caused the death*, and not after the death itself, or the reporting of the accident, or the requesting of any other samples. Answers A, B and C are therefore incorrect. This will presumably present practical problems where the injured person dies *after* the 18 hours elapses.

Question 9

Answer **B** — Statement 1 is incorrect. Under s. 3A(1) of the Road Traffic Act 1988, a person commits the offence by driving a *mechanically propelled vehicle* on a road or public place.

However, this statement is amended slightly under s. 3A(3), which states that offences under s. 3A(1)(b) (driver exceeding the prescribed limit) and 3A(1)(c) (driver failing to provide a specimen for analysis) may only be committed by the driver of a *motor vehicle*. The remaining offence under s. 3A(1)(a) (driver unfit through drink or drugs) is the only one under this section that can be committed by the driver of a mechanically propelled vehicle.

There seems no obvious reason for the legislation to have been written this way, other than the fact that the offences under s. 3A follow those under ss. 4 and 5 of the Act (offences committed by the driver of a *mechanically propelled vehicle* and a *motor vehicle* respectively).

Statement 2 is correct — the offence may be committed on a road or other public place.

Consequently, answers A, C and D are incorrect.

Question 10

Answer **D** — Statement 1 is incorrect. Under s. 38(7) of the Road Traffic Act 1988, a failure by a person to observe a provision of the Highway Code may be used in civil proceedings *or* criminal cases to establish or negative any liability as to their driving.

Statement 2 is also incorrect; the braking distances shown in the Highway Code are *not* admissible in proving speeding cases in court, as they amount to *hearsay* (*R* v *Chadwick* [1975] Crim LR 105).

Consequently, answers A, B and C are incorrect.

Question 11

Answer **C** — Under s. 172(2) of the Road Traffic Act 1988, where the driver of a vehicle has committed an offence to which the section applies (this includes ss. 3 and 170 (accidents)), the keeper of the vehicle shall give information as to the identity of the driver as required by or on behalf of a chief officer of police.

There is no mention of a person having to be authorised to make such a request on behalf of the chief officer and therefore it can be assumed that as Constable Pierce is acting in the course of his duties, he is acting on behalf of the chief officer. Answer D is therefore incorrect.

When a request is made by post, the keeper has 28 days in which to reply. The 1988 Act does not state that *all* requests must be made by post and answer B is therefore incorrect. On the contrary, the case of *Lowe* v *Lester* [1987] RTR 30 indicates that requests may be made verbally, and the information must be provided within a reasonable time, which may in the prevailing circumstances mean *immediately*. Therefore, answer A is incorrect.

Question 12

Answer **B** — There is no special exemption for emergency drivers with regard to standards of driving (*R* v *O'Toole* (1971) 55 Cr App R 206), and they will be judged against the standards of care which apply to all drivers. There is an exemption which allows emergency drivers to pass through red lights under the Traffic Signs Regulations and General Directions 1994 (SI 1994 No. 1519), reg. 33. However, this *does not* exempt emergency drivers from having to drive with due care and attention. Answer A is therefore incorrect.

Answer C is incorrect because of the case of *DPP* v *Harris* [1995] RTR 100, where the driver of a police surveillance vehicle following a suspect drove through a red light. The court held that even though the suspects were being followed to the scene of an armed robbery, the seriousness of the circumstances did not provide an exemption.

Answer D is incorrect (and consequently answer B is correct), because of a recent ruling in the case of *S (A Child)* v *Keyse* (2001) 151 NLJ 817. There, it was held that police and other emergency service drivers were entitled to expect other road users to take note of the signs of their approach (e.g. sirens and flashing lights) and, where appropriate, to react accordingly. Therefore, this decision may provide a defence in the circumstances outlined in the question.

Question 13

Answer **B** — The defence(s) of *duress* and *necessity* will apply to cases of dangerous driving, careless and inconsiderate driving *and* driving while disqualified (*R* v *Martin* [1989] RTR 63 and *R* v *Backshall* [1998]

1 WLR 1506). Answer D is therefore incorrect. The defence of duress will only apply where the defendant was forced to commit an offence to avoid death or serious injury (*R* v *Conway* [1989] RTR 35). The defence *will not* apply in cases of criminal damage or where criminal damage has been threatened, no matter how serious. Answers A and C are therefore incorrect.

3 NOTICES OF INTENDED PROSECUTION

STUDY PREPARATION

Like much road traffic legislation, the law governing Notice of Intended Prosecution is concerned with procedural detail. Once you know which offences are generally covered by the NIP procedure, you then need to learn the procedure required for proper service to be accepted by the courts and any exceptions provided for.

Understanding the purpose behind NIPs will help you in learning all this important procedural detail.

QUESTIONS

Question 1

Constable DALTON was following a car being driven by a person whom he recognised as being GIBSON. GIBSON failed to stop for the officer and following a pursuit, Constable DALTON lost sight of the car. The officer knew GIBSON's home address and attended there straight away, in order to report him for driving without due care and attention. There was no reply at the house. Constable DALTON eventually caught up with GIBSON two days later.

What action should the officer now take, to comply with s. 1 of the Road Traffic Offenders Act 1988 (notice of intended prosecution (NIP))?

[A]   Issue a verbal NIP personally to GIBSON there and then.
[B]   Send a written NIP or summons to GIBSON within 12 days.
[C]   Send both a written NIP and summons to GIBSON within 14 days.
[D]   Send a written NIP or summons to GIBSON within 14 days.

Question 2

Which of the following statements, if either, is/are correct in relation to notices of intended prosecution (NIP)?

1.   If a verbal warning is given, and the defendant claims not to have understood the warning, it is for the defendant to prove that he or she did not understand.
2.   When an offence is committed partly within the jurisdiction of two different courts, it must be heard in the court where the first offence took place.

[A]   Statement 1 only.
[B]   Statement 2 only.
[C]   Both statements.
[D]   Neither statement.

Question 3

HAWKLEY was responsible for failing to stop after an accident in a supermarket car park, when he damaged another car and drove off. A witness took his registration number and reported the accident to Constable DAVIES. The officer sent a notice of intended prosecution (NIP), to HAWKLEY's address as shown on PNC. However, HAWKLEY had moved. HAWKLEY was traced two months later, and when interviewed, stated he had never received the NIP.

What effect would the failure to serve the NIP have on any future prosecution against HAWKLEY?

[A] None, as HAWKLEY was at fault for the failure of the service.
[B] The NIP was not served in time and therefore the case cannot proceed.
[C] None, a NIP was not required as the offence occurred at the time of an accident.
[D] None, a NIP was not required as the accident did not occur on a road.

Question 4

In which of the following scenarios will a notice of intended prosecution (NIP) have been correctly served under s. 1 of the Road Traffic Offenders Act 1988?

1. A NIP was served personally by the officer in the case on the defendant's common law husband.
2. The defendant was on holiday for six weeks. The officer in the case was aware of this but still served a written NIP to the defendant's home address, while the defendant was away.
3. An officer gave a verbal NIP to a motorist, who later claimed that the officer had not specified what offence he was being prosecuted for and was only told that he had committed a 'speeding offence'.

[A] Scenarios 2 and 3 only.
[B] All three scenarios.
[C] Scenarios 1 and 3 only.
[D] Scenarios 1 and 2 only.

ANSWERS

Question 1

Answer **B** — Under s. 1 of the Road Traffic Offenders Act 1988, before certain offences can be prosecuted, the defendant must have *either* been warned of the possibility of prosecution at the time of the offence, *or* served with a summons (or charged) within 14 days of the offence *or* a notice of intended prosecution (NIP) must have been sent to the registered keeper within 14 days of the offence.

Answer A is incorrect as a verbal NIP may only be given at the time of the offence. If this is not possible, the prosecution is able to send a written one to the keeper's last known address.

Answer C is incorrect as there is no requirement to send both the summons and the written NIP within 14 days; one will suffice. Answer C is also incorrect, as is answer D, because two days have already elapsed since the incident, and the written NIP (or summons) must be sent within 14 days of the *offence committed.*

Question 2

Answer **D** — Statement 1 is incorrect. If a verbal warning is given, it must be shown that the defendant understood it (*Gibson* v *Dalton* [1980] RTR 410). Proof that the defendant understood the warning would lie with the *prosecution.*

Statement 2 is also incorrect. When an offence is committed partly within the jurisdiction of two different courts, it may be heard in *either* court (*Kennet DC* v *Faroq, The Times,* 16 October 1998).

Consequently, answers A, B and C are incorrect.

Question 3

Answer **A** — Section 2(1) of the Road Traffic Offenders Act 1988 states that a NIP does not need to be served if at the time or immediately afterwards and owing to the presence of the motor vehicle concerned *on a road* an accident occurred. This means that where an accident occurs on a road, a NIP is not required for a due care offence; however, where an accident occurs in a public place a NIP *will be* required. Answers C and D are therefore incorrect.

A notice must be served on the defendant within 14 days of the offence, if it was not given verbally at the time. However, under s. 2(3) of the 1988 Act, if the defendant contributes to the failure to serve the NIP, then that will not be a bar to his or her conviction. Answer B is therefore incorrect.

Question 4

Answer **B** — All three of the scenarios are based on decided cases, where the court agreed that the provisions of s. 1(1) of the Road Traffic Act 1988 had been complied with.

Scenario 1 is based on the case of *Hosier* v *Goodall* [1962] 1 All ER 30, where it was decided that a notice served on the defendant's spouse or partner was sufficient.

Scenario 2 is based on the case of *Phipps* v *McCormick* [1972] Crim LR 540, where it was held that if the defendant is not at his or her home address, for instance because he or she is in hospital or on holiday, service to his or her last known address will suffice, even if the police are aware of that fact.

Scenario 3 comes from the case of *Pope* v *Clarke* [1953] 2 All ER 704, where it was held that a purpose of the notice is to alert the defendant of the likelihood of prosecution. It is not necessary to specify which offence is being considered; it is enough that the defendant is made aware of the *nature* of the offence.

Consequently, answers A, C and D are incorrect.

4 ACCIDENTS

STUDY PREPARATION

The law relating to road traffic accidents is primarily concerned with obligations on the drivers involved and the offences for failing to comply with those obligations.

The most important bit of this subject is knowing what amounts to an 'accident'. You need to be able to recognise from the fact pattern of a question whether an 'accident' has happened. Then you need to know what obligations the law imposes and upon whom. You also need to know any offences which may apply, along with the attendant police powers.

QUESTIONS

Question 1

BENNETT was involved in a road traffic accident, while driving his employer's van. He drove into the rear of a car at a set of traffic lights. BENNETT was asked by the driver of the other vehicle for his name and address only. BENNETT gave his own name, but gave his employer's address as he was driving a works vehicle.

Has BENNETT complied with s. 170(2) of the Road Traffic Act 1988 (duty to stop and give details) in these circumstances?

[A]   No, he should also have given the name of the owner of the vehicle to the other driver.

[B]   No, he should also have given the name of the owner of the vehicle, and the registration number to the other driver.

[C]   Yes, he has complied fully with the requirements of the Act in these circumstances.

[D]   No, he should have given his own address to the other driver, not his employer's.

Question 2

CAWTHORN was driving his car and towing a trailer, when he stopped at a shop on the brow of a hill. While he was inside the shop, the coupling which fixed the trailer to the car broke. The trailer rolled down the hill and collided with a parked car causing damage to it.

What obligation does CAWTHORN have to exchange details with the driver of the parked vehicle in these circumstances?

[A]   None, as he was not to blame for the accident.

[B]   He has an obligation to stop and exchange details with the owner.

[C]   None, as he was not driving a vehicle at the time of the accident.

[D]   None, as the trailer is not a mechanically propelled vehicle.

Question 3

CUTTER was involved in an accident in a multi-storey car park, which was open to the public at the time. CUTTER was driving out of a parking space in his van when he scraped the side of a parked car. CUTTER failed to stop after the accident; however a witness noted his registration number. When he was traced by the police, CUTTER stated that he hadn't stopped, as he was unaware of the accident.

Who would have responsibility for proving or disproving that CUTTER was unaware of the accident?

[A]   The defence must show on the balance of probabilities he was unaware of the accident.
[B]   The prosecution must show beyond reasonable doubt he would have been aware of the accident.
[C]   The defence must show beyond reasonable doubt he was unaware of the accident.
[D]   The question is not relevant; there was no requirement to stop after the accident as it did not occur on a road.

Question 4

Which of the following statements, if either, is/are correct in relation to s. 170 of the Road Traffic Act 1988?

1.   'Injury' for the purposes of the section will *not* include psychological harm.
2.   If a driver fails to stop after an accident and fails to report it, he or she will commit two offences.

[A]   Statement 1 only.
[B]   Statement 2 only.
[C]   Both statements.
[D]   Neither statement.

Question 5

BATES was driving in the early hours of the morning, in a built up area, when he collided with a parked car while negotiating a bend. Damage was caused to the parked car. BATES stopped his car, but as it was so late, there was nobody about.

What must BATES now do, in relation to the damaged car?

[A] Remain at the scene until someone arrives to give details to.
[B] Report the accident to the police within 24 hours.
[C] Make enquiries of his own to find the owner before he leaves.
[D] Report the accident to the police as soon as practicable.

Question 6

While driving his car, DAWSON was involved in a road traffic accident with a motor cycle being ridden by WINTER. WINTER suffered cuts and grazes as a result. The drivers exchanged details and WINTER asked DAWSON for his insurance certificate. DAWSON did not have it with him, but gave WINTER the name of his insurance company and promised to show him the certificate the next day.

Has DAWSON complied with the requirements of s. 170 of the Road Traffic Act 1988 in these circumstances?

[A] Yes, he is not obliged to produce his insurance certificate to another driver, providing he gives the name of his insurance company.
[B] No, he must report the accident to the police as soon as reasonably practicable, and produce his insurance certificate within seven days.
[C] No, he must report the accident to the police as soon as reasonably practicable, and produce his insurance certificate at the same time.
[D] Yes, provided he produces his insurance certificate to WINTER within 24 hours.

ANSWERS

Question 1

Answer **C** — Under s. 170(2) of the Road Traffic Act 1988, the driver of a vehicle involved in a road traffic accident must stop and *if required to do so* by some person having reasonable grounds, give his or her name and address and also the name and address of the owner of the vehicle, and the registration mark of the vehicle.

Because the driver of the other vehicle did not ask for the name of the owner and the registration mark, Bennett commits no offence by failing to give them. Answers A and B are therefore incorrect.

It has been held that, as the reason for the requirement to 'exchange details' is to allow future communications between parties, the address of the driver's solicitor would satisfy the requirements of s. 170(2) (*R* v *McCarthy*, *The Times*, 8 January 1999). Answer D is therefore incorrect.

Question 2

Answer **B** — It has been held that even though a driver may not have been to blame for an accident, he or she will still attract the duties imposed by s. 170 of the Road Traffic Act 1988 (*Harding* v *Price* [1948] 1 All ER 283). Answer A is therefore incorrect.

If there has been a break from driving, and an accident occurs while the driver is away from the vehicle, he or she will still be required to fulfil the obligations of s. 170 (*Cawthorn* v *DPP* [2000] RTR 45). In this case, even though the driver was not directly responsible for the accident (the passenger had let off the handbrake), there was still a requirement to comply with s. 170. Answer C is incorrect as there is no requirement for a person to be driving at the time of the accident.

Answer D is incorrect as s. 170(1) requires the driver to stop and exchange details when damage was caused to another vehicle by his or her own vehicle, or a trailer being drawn by it.

Question 3

Answer **A** — the case of *Cutter* v *Eagle Star Insurance Co. Ltd* [1998] 4 All ER 417 changed the requirements under s. 170 of the Road Traffic Act 1988. Prior to this case, an accident was not 'reportable' unless it occurred on a road. The section has now been extended to include 'public places'. Since the car park was open to any member of the public, it was a public place and covered by s. 170. Answer D is therefore incorrect.

When a driver alleges he or she was unaware that an accident had taken place, it is for the defence to show *on the balance of probabilities* that this was the case (*Selby* v *Chief Constable of Avon and Somerset* [1988] RTR 216. Answers B and C are therefore incorrect.

Question 4

Answer **B** — Statement 1 is incorrect. Injury under s. 170 of the Road Traffic Act 1988 has been held to include shock, and given recent developments in the area of assaults (e.g. *R* v *Ireland* [1997] 3 WLR 534 and *R* v *Chan-Fook* [1994] 1 WLR 689), it would appear that psychological harm might amount to injury also.

Statement 2 is correct. If a driver fails to stop and fails to report an accident, he or she *will* commit two offences (*Roper* v *Sullivan* [1978] RTR 181).

Consequently, answers A, C and D are incorrect.

Question 5

Answer **D** — Under s. 170(2) of the Road Traffic Act 1988 a driver is required to stop at the scene and remain there for long enough to allow anyone having a right or reason for doing so to ask for information from the driver (*Lee* v *Knapp* [1967] 2 QB 442). It does not require the driver to make his or her own enquiries to find such a person (*Mutton* v *Bates* [1984] RTR 256). Answer C is therefore incorrect.

The driver is also under a duty to stay with his or her vehicle for a reasonable time for the above requirements (*Ward* v *Rawson* [1978] RTR 498). Answer A is incorrect as there is no requirement to wait until someone happens to arrive.

If a driver does not give details at the scene for whatever reason, he or she is required to report the accident to a police officer or at a police station. This must be done *as soon as reasonably practicable* (and it will be for the court to decide what is reasonable), and in any case within 24 hours.

This *does not* give the driver 24 hours to report the accident — and in most circumstances there is no reason for an accident not to be reported straight away because of the availability of police officers 24 hours a day. Answer B is therefore incorrect.

Question 6

Answer **C** — If a driver is involved in an accident where injury is caused to another person, he or she must, at the time of the accident, produce a certificate of insurance to a constable *or* any person having reasonable grounds for requiring it (s. 170(5) of the Road Traffic Act 1988). Answer A is therefore incorrect.

If the driver does not produce his or her insurance certificate as required above, he or she *must* report the accident to the police *and* produce an insurance certificate as soon as practicable, and in any case within 24 hours (s. 170(6)).

Answer D is incorrect as once a driver fails to produce a certificate at the scene to the other driver, the requirement moves to reporting the accident and producing the certificate to the police.

Answer B is incorrect as the requirement is to report the accident *and* produce the insurance certificate as soon as practicable and within 24 hours. Under s. 170(7) of the 1988 Act, a person will escape prosecution for failing to produce insurance at the time of the accident, or later at the police station, if he or she produces it within seven days from the accident (usually as a result of the issue of an HORT1). Therefore, although answer B may appear correct, the *first* process must be to report the accident and produce the certificate as soon as practicable.

5 DRINK DRIVING

STUDY PREPARATION

This is a big one. The areas of law and procedure covered in this chapter are extensive. You will need to know the elements of each of the main drink driving offences first. Entwined with those offences are a range of police powers such as the powers to require breath samples. Failure or refusal to comply with such requirements can lead to further offences and further powers.

It is sometimes helpful to divide this subject area into roadside, police station and hospital procedures.

The evidential issues are also important and there is a great deal of established case law to clarify this area of the legislation.

QUESTIONS

Question 1

Constable PITROLA was stopped by GRANGER, who had seen a man in a pub earlier, drinking heavily. The man was now sitting in a car outside the pub and GRANGER feared he might drive. As Constable PITROLA approached the car he saw HART sitting in the driver's seat. HART saw the officer and locked all the doors, refusing to open them again.

Would Constable PITROLA have a power to enter the vehicle by force to deal with HART under s. 4 of the Road Traffic Act 1988 (in charge of or unfit to drive a vehicle)?

[A] No, GRANGER's suspicion that HART is drunk is not sufficient to provide reasonable suspicion to enter the vehicle.
[B] Yes, in order to breathalise HART, on reasonable suspicion that he is unfit to drive through drink.
[C] Yes, in order to arrest HART, on reasonable suspicion that he is unfit to drive through drink.
[D] No, as the power provided under this section is to enter a premises and not a vehicle.

Question 2

Section 4(3) of the Road Traffic Act 1988 provides a defence for a person charged with an offence under s. 4 of the Act; provided it was unlikely he or she would drive a vehicle while unfit.

In relation to this defence, which of the following statements is correct?

[A] The onus is on the defence to prove this fact and the court will not take into account any injury to the defendant or damage to the vehicle.
[B] The onus is on the prosecution to prove this fact and the court will take into account any injury to the defendant or damage to the vehicle.
[C] The onus is on the defence to prove this fact and the court will take into account any injury to the defendant or damage to the vehicle.
[D] The onus is on the prosecution to prove this fact and the court will not take into account any injury to the defendant or damage to the vehicle.

Question 3

Constable McDONALD arrested ROFF for driving while disqualified. On the way to the station, ROFF began acting in a peculiar manner. When they arrived at the custody office, Constable McDONALD could not detect any signs that ROFF had been drinking. A short while later, the officer received information from a colleague that several canisters of butane gas had been found in ROFF's car.

Would Constable McDONALD now be entitled to arrest ROFF for an offence contrary to s. 4 of the Road Traffic Act 1988?

[A]   No, as butane gas is not a 'drug', and it is unlikely that the prosecution will be able show the quantity of it in ROFF's body.
[B]   No, because the officer formed the suspicion that ROFF was intoxicated after he had stopped driving his vehicle.
[C]   No, because a constable may only arrest a person under this section when they are committing the offence.
[D]   Yes, Constable McDonald has reason to suspect that ROFF has committed an offence under s. 4 of the Act.

Question 4

Constable SIER was on foot patrol one night, when a vehicle drove past him with a defective headlamp. Constable SIER recognised the driver as being ERSKINE and contacted his control room to ask for the vehicle to be stopped by another officer. Constable WHEELAN was on patrol in uniform about 20 minutes later, when he saw ERSKINE walking along. The vehicle was nowhere in sight.

Would Constable WHEELAN have the power to require a breath test from ERSKINE in these circumstances?

[A]   Yes, but only if he suspects ERSKINE has alcohol in his body.
[B]   Yes, because he has committed a moving traffic offence.
[C]   No, because he did not see ERSKINE driving himself.
[D]   No, because ERSKINE is no longer driving.

Question 5

Constable COURT was conducting her first breath test procedure, having stopped KAY, who was driving with a defective light. During the test, Constable COURT failed to hold down a button on the breath test device for the recommended amount of time. However, the reading still showed a positive breath result and Constable COURT arrested KAY.

Has Constable COURT acted correctly in these circumstances?

[A] Yes, Constable COURT has acted correctly in the circumstances and the arrest is lawful.
[B] No, the arrest is unlawful, as Constable COURT made a mistake with the procedure.
[C] No, the arrest is unlawful, but this would not affect the result of the case if KAY provided a positive sample at the station.
[D] No, the arrest is unlawful, and KAY should have been made to take the test again.

Question 6

Constable TAYLOR was called to an accident in a shopping centre car park, which was open to the public. SINGH had reversed his car into the path of a dumper truck being driven by WALSH. WALSH was working on an adjacent building site and the dumper truck he was driving was not manufactured for use on roads.

From whom, if anyone, may Constable TAYLOR require a breath test, in these circumstances?

[A] SINGH only, provided she suspects he has alcohol in his body.
[B] Neither driver, as the accident did not occur on a road.
[C] Both drivers, as they have been involved in an accident.
[D] SINGH only, whether or not she suspects he has alcohol in his body.

Question 7

Detective Constable PRINCE was in plain clothes, driving an unmarked police vehicle, when he saw DART, who was driving a motor car, collide with a pedal cyclist. The cycle was damaged as a result of the accident. DC PRINCE stopped to assist and as he was speaking to DART, he could smell intoxicants on his breath. DC PRINCE asked DART to provide a specimen of breath, but he had no device with him, nor did he have a radio to call for one. DC PRINCE asked DART to accompany him to the nearest police station to provide the specimen.

Has DC PRINCE acted correctly in these circumstances?

[A] No, he was not in uniform and had no power to demand a breath test.
[B] No, he should have waited until he was at the station to request the specimen.
[C] Yes, he has acted correctly in these circumstances.
[D] No, the specimen should have been provided at the scene of the accident.

Question 8

Constable MAY has stopped LENNARD, who had driven through a 'No Entry' sign late at night. Constable MAY asked LENNARD to supply a specimen of breath. LENNARD stated that he was unable to do so, as he had recently had heart surgery and the test may cause him to be seriously ill.

Would Constable MAY be entitled to arrest LENNARD for failing to supply a sample of breath?

[A] Yes, any person who refuses to supply a breath test may be arrested.
[B] Yes, but only if she suspects LENNARD has alcohol in his body.
[C] No, no further action should be taken because of LENNARD's illness.
[D] Yes, provided she suspects that LENNARD is over the prescribed limit.

Question 9

BALL drove his car into a garden wall and without stopping, he made his way home. He was alone in the car and no other people were involved. Constable DAWE arrived at the scene and, following a PNC check, attended BALL's home address. Constable DAWE found BALL in the front garden of his house and asked him for a sample of breath, as the officer suspected he had been involved in a road traffic accident. BALL refused and was arrested by the officer. BALL refused to go with Constable DAWE and told him to leave his property.

Does Constable DAWE have the power to continue with his arrest now that he has become a trespasser?

[A] Yes, BALL was arrested before Constable DAWE became a trespasser.

[B] Yes, Constable DAWE had a power to enter premises, as BALL had been involved in an accident.

[C] No, the arrest was unlawful, as Constable DAWE was trespassing as soon as he entered the garden.

[D] No, Constable DAWE has now become a trespasser and must leave the property.

Question 10

Section 6(6) of the Road Traffic Act 1988 provides a power of entry for a constable in certain circumstances.

Which of the following statements accurately sets out the relevant criteria that must apply before the power exists?

[A] Reasonable belief that an accident has taken place; reasonable belief that the person was the driver; reasonable suspicion that it involved injury; reasonable suspicion that the person is on the premises.

[B] Reasonable suspicion that an accident has taken place; reasonable suspicion that the person was the driver; knowledge that it involved injury; reasonable suspicion that the driver is on the premises.

[C] Knowledge that an accident has taken place; reasonable belief that the person was the driver; reasonable suspicion that it involved injury; knowledge that the person is on the premises.

[D] Knowledge that an accident has taken place; reasonable belief that the person was the driver; reasonable suspicion that it involved injury; reasonable suspicion that the person is on the premises.

Question 11

In relation to s. 7 of the Road Traffic Act 1988 (provision of specimens for analysis), which of the following statements, if either, is/are correct?

1. A requirement under s. 7 for a breath specimen may only be made at a police station or a hospital.
2. The requirement under s. 7 may be made of more than one person in respect of the same vehicle.

[A] Statement 1 only.
[B] Statement 2 only.
[C] Both statements.
[D] Neither statement.

Question 12

Sergeant COWLEY was conducting the station breath test procedure for CATTON. CATTON was so drunk that Sergeant COWLEY feared he did not understand the procedure. As a precaution, Sergeant COWLEY called a police doctor to examine CATTON, believing there might be a medical reason for not providing a specimen of breath.

Has Sergeant COWLEY acted lawfully in these circumstances?

[A] No, he should have consulted the police doctor before deciding there was a medical reason preventing CATTON from providing a sample.

[B] No, he did not have reasonable cause to believe CATTON had a medical reason preventing him from providing a sample.

[C] Yes, Sergeant COWLEY has acted lawfully in these circumstances because of CATTON's condition.

[D] No, CATTON's drunkenness would not be a medical reason, which would prevent him from providing a sample.

Question 13

Sergeant SWEENEY was conducting the station breath test procedure in relation to DENNY. DENNY provided one specimen of breath, which was over the prescribed limit. However, before he could provide a second specimen, the machine malfunctioned and Sergeant SWEENEY was unable to complete the procedure.

What action should Sergeant SWEENEY have taken in order to complete the station procedure?

[A] Request that DENNY provides a sample of blood or urine, and use that reading, together with the breath test reading as evidence.

[B] Charge DENNY with driving with excess alcohol, using the one reading as evidence that he was over the limit.

[C] The only option available to Sergeant SWEENEY is to request that DENNY provides a sample of blood to replace the reading.

[D] Sergeant SWEENEY may transfer DENNY to another station if there is another machine available.

Question 14

In which of the scenarios below, if any, will the custody officer have acted **incorrectly**, in respect of a requirement made under s. 7 of the Road Traffic Act 1988? (In each case the defendant has been arrested for providing a positive roadside breath test.)

1. The custody officer has requested a blood sample from THYNNE instead of two specimens of breath because the breath test machine is defective.
2. The custody officer has required BERRY to provide a blood sample for medical reasons, and has transferred him to another station, where a doctor is available.
3. The custody officer has requested a blood sample from KELLIHER, as there is no trained officer available to take specimens of breath.

[A] None of the above.
[B] Scenarios 1 and 3 only.
[C] Scenario 2 only.
[D] Scenario 2 and 3 only.

Question 15

COLE was arrested for failing to provide a roadside breath test. On his arrival at the police station, COLE provided two samples of breath. Both readings were very low. However, the custody officer, Sergeant WONG, believed that COLE may have taken drugs as he was exhibiting similar behaviour to a drunken person.

What would be the correct course of action for Sergeant WONG to take in these circumstances?

[A] Consult a doctor, who must confirm in writing that COLE's behaviour is due to his taking drugs and then request a sample of blood or urine.
[B] Request a blood or urine sample from COLE and then call a doctor to take either the blood sample or urine sample.
[C] Consult a doctor, who must confirm verbally that COLE's behaviour is due to his taking drugs and then request a sample of blood or urine.
[D] Request a blood or urine sample from COLE and then call a doctor to take the sample, if it is blood, or take the sample himself if it is urine.

Question 16

Under s.7(4) of the Road Traffic Act 1988, a specimen of blood or urine may be required from a person in custody.

In relation to this provision, who will decide which specimen is to be obtained from such a person?

[A] It will always be the officer's decision, and there is no requirement to consult on this issue.
[B] It will always be the officer's decision, unless the driver objects; then a doctor will rule on the validity of the objection.
[C] It will always be the officer's decision, but he or she may take into account any objections made by the driver before arriving at the decision.
[D] It will always be the officer's decision, unless the driver objects; then it will be a joint decision in consultation with a doctor.

Question 17

When a constable is requesting the provision of a sample under s. 7 of the Road Traffic Act 1988, a warning must be given to the person in custody.

In relation to the warning, which of the following statements, if either, is/are correct?

1. The warning under s. 7 need only be given in cases where the samples requested are blood or urine; it is not required where a breath sample is requested.
2. The warning under s. 7 must be given in every case by the same officer who makes the request for the relevant sample.

[A] Statement 1 only.
[B] Statement 2 only.
[C] Both statements.
[D] Neither statement.

Question 18

KHAN has provided two specimens of breath during the station breath test procedure, the readings being 49 and 50 respectively. Sergeant WILSON informed KHAN that he could replace the samples with blood or urine. KHAN stated that he would prefer not to give blood, as he had a fear of needles. Sergeant WILSON has been informed that a doctor is available by telephone only and will not attend immediately.

What action should Sergeant WILSON now take in respect of KHAN?

[A] Speak to the doctor on the telephone and proceed as advised by him or her.
[B] Request a sample of blood if necessary; a fear of needles is not a medical reason for not giving blood.
[C] Take a sample of urine from KHAN, as the choice is his as to which sample may be taken.
[D] Wait until the doctor arrives and proceed as advised by him or her; such advice may not be taken by telephone.

Question 19

In relation to the provision of a specimen of blood by a person under s. 8 of the Road Traffic Act 1988 (following the provision of two specimens of breath), which of the following statements, if either, is/are true?

1. When a fault occurs, which leads to a blood specimen being unsuitable, the prosecution may use the original breath specimens to prove the person was over the limit.
2. A driver should be given the opportunity to state any medical reasons why blood should not be taken, but failing to give him or her that opportunity will not necessarily lead to the failure of the case.

[A] Statement 1 only.
[B] Statement 2 only.
[C] Both statements.
[D] Neither statement.

Question 20

Sergeant DONELLY was conducting the station breath test procedure for BEECH, who had provided one sample of breath. However, BEECH stated that he was tired, and fell asleep before providing a second sample. Sergeant DONELLY tried to wake BEECH, without success, and in the end placed him in a cell. BEECH was later charged with driving with excess alcohol, based on the reading provided, which was 150 microgrammes of alcohol in 100 millilitres of breath.

Has Sergeant DONELLY acted correctly in these circumstances?

[A] Yes, Sergeant DONELLY has acted correctly in these circumstances as BEECH has driven with excess alcohol.
[B] No, BEECH should have been charged with failing to provide a sample, but his drunken condition may provide a defence.
[C] No, BEECH should have been given the opportunity to provide a sample of blood or urine when he was sober enough.
[D] No, BEECH should have been charged with failing to provide a sample and would have no defence arising from his drunken condition.

Question 21

In which of the following scenarios has it been held that a person does **not** have a reasonable excuse for failing to provide a specimen under s. 7 of the Road Traffic Act 1988?

1. The defendant refused to supply a specimen because he or she believed that the officer did not have the authority to ask for one.
2. The defendant refused to supply a specimen because he or she could not understand what was being said due to a language barrier.
3. The defendant refused to supply a specimen until he or she had spoken to a solicitor.
4. The defendant refused to supply a specimen until he or she had read the Codes of Practice under the Police and Criminal Evidence Act 1984.

[A] All of the above.
[B] Scenarios 1, 2 and 4 only.
[C] Scenarios 3 and 4 only.
[D] Scenarios 1, 3 and 4 only.

Question 22

In which of the following scenarios, if either, will the person have failed to provide a specimen for analysis, without 'reasonable excuse', under s. 7(6) of the Road Traffic Act 1988?

1. HIGGINS has consented to provide a specimen of blood, but only if it is taken from his left arm.
2. DICKESON consented to providing a specimen of urine, but was only able to urinate once. He has refused to provide a second sample, stating that the one he has provided may be split in two.

[A] Scenario 1 only.
[B] Scenario 2 only.
[C] Both scenarios.
[D] Neither scenario.

Question 23

MILLARD was charged with causing death by careless driving, whilst unfit to drive through drugs. MILLARD proposed to introduce evidence in court to prove that she had not been under the influence of drugs at the time of the alleged offence. MILLARD contested that she had taken drugs after she had ceased to drive her car, and was no longer in charge of it.

What effect will this have on the court's ability to make an assumption, under s. 15 of the Road Traffic Offenders Act 1988, that the proportion of drugs in MILLARD's body was the same at the time of the accident, as when she later provided the sample?

[A] The court will only take into account any sample provided by MILLARD, if the prosecution can discredit her evidence.
[B] None, the court would not have been able to make that assumption as MILLARD was not under the influence of alcohol.
[C] None, the assumption under s. 15 does not apply to the offence that MILLARD is alleged to have committed.
[D] None, only the prosecution may introduce such evidence and since they have not, the court must take into account the sample.

Question 24

Section 15(5) of the Road Traffic Offenders Act 1988, deals with the provision of a specimen to the accused, which has been taken from him or her.

In relation to the provision of such a sample, which of the following statements will be correct?

[A] It must be provided in every case to the defendant at the time it was taken, after it has been divided in his or her presence.
[B] It must be provided when requested by the defendant, not necessarily at the time it was taken, and it need not be divided in his or her presence.
[C] It must be provided in every case to the defendant at the time it was taken, but it need not be divided in his or her presence.
[D] It must be provided when requested by the defendant at the time it was taken, after it has been divided in his or her presence.

Question 25

Section 16 of the Road Traffic Offenders Act 1988 deals with documentary evidence in relation to the taking of specimens of breath, blood or urine.

In relation to this section, which of the following statements, if either, is/are correct?

1. It is for the prosecution to prove beyond reasonable doubt that the defendant consented to a sample of blood being taken.
2. Where a person has supplied two specimens of breath, he or she must be supplied with a copy of the certificate produced, signed by the officer producing it.

[A] Statement 1 only.
[B] Statement 2 only.
[C] Both statements.
[D] Neither statement.

Question 26

NEWMAN is in custody and is suspected of being unfit to drive through taking drugs. NEWMAN has provided a specimen of blood, which the custody officer, Sergeant BURKE, intends to submit for analysis. NEWMAN will not be charged until the results of the analysis are known and, therefore, Sergeant BURKE intends to release him on bail for the period. However, NEWMAN has stated his intention to drive when released. Sergeant BURKE suspects that NEWMAN would still be unfit if he were to drive a motor vehicle on a road.

What does s. 10 of the Road Traffic Act 1988 say, in relation to the action Sergeant BURKE should take, if she decides to detain NEWMAN further until he is fit to drive a motor vehicle on a road?

[A] No further action need be taken; Sergeant Burke may make this decision herself.
[B] Sergeant BURKE may seek advice from a doctor, and must act on any advice given.
[C] Sergeant BURKE may not detain NEWMAN under this section, as he has not been charged or reported with an offence.
[D] Sergeant BURKE *must* seek advice from a doctor, and must act on any advice given.

Question 27

ASKEW, having been involved in a road traffic accident where she received injuries, has been taken to hospital. Constable LEE is dealing with the accident and has attended the hospital to interview ASKEW and require her to provide a sample of breath.

In relation to the requirement under s. 9 of the Road Traffic Act 1988, which of the following statements is correct?

[A] Constable LEE may make the requirement, but the sample may not be taken unless a doctor at the hospital has been consulted.
[B] Constable LEE may not make the requirement unless the doctor in immediate charge of ASKEW has been consulted.
[C] Constable LEE may not make the requirement while ASKEW is a patient at the hospital.
[D] The requirement may be made, but the sample may not be taken until the doctor in immediate charge of ASKEW has been consulted.

Question 28

WEBBER was at a hospital, having been involved in a road traffic accident. Having consulted with WEBBER's doctor, Constable O'SHEA required WEBBER to provide a specimen of breath, but she refused. Constable O'SHEA arrested WEBBER for failing to provide a specimen. After further consultation with the doctor, Constable O'SHEA asked WEBBER to supply a specimen of blood.

Has Constable O'SHEA complied with the requirements of s. 9 of the Road Traffic Act 1988?

[A] No, because WEBBER was under arrest, the request for blood should have been made at a police station.
[B] No, he should not have arrested WEBBER while she was still a patient at the hospital.
[C] Yes, as the doctor has agreed to both specimens being requested, he has complied with the Act.
[D] Yes, but there was no need to ask permission on the second occasion, as permission had already been granted.

ANSWERS

Question 1

Answer **C** — Section 4(6) of the Road Traffic Act 1988 provides that a constable may arrest a person without warrant if he or she has reasonable cause to suspect that they have committed an offence under s. 4. For the purpose of *arresting* a person under the power conferred by s. 4(6), a constable may enter, if need be by force, *any place* where that person is or with reasonable cause is suspected to be (s. 4(7)). Answer B is incorrect as the power is provided to enter to *arrest* a person, not to breathalise. Answer D is incorrect as the power is available to enter any *place* where the person is.

Evidence of impairment must be produced by the prosecution, and that evidence may be provided by a 'lay' witness, provided that witness is not required to give expert testimony or to comment on the defendant's ability to drive (*Bradford* v *Wilson* [1983] 78 Cr App R 77). Answer A is therefore incorrect.

Question 2

Answer **A** — Simply, the onus is with the *defendant* to show he or she was unlikely to drive the vehicle while still intoxicated. The court will *not* take into account any injury to the defendant or damage to the vehicle when determining whether he or she was likely to drive the vehicle. Answers B, C and D are therefore incorrect.

Question 3

Answer **D** — 'Drugs' for the purpose of s. 4 of the Road Traffic Act 1988 will include any intoxicant other than alcohol (s. 11), and will include *toluene* found in some glues (*Bradford* v *Wilson* (1983) 78 Cr App R 77). As the effects of butane gas can be 'intoxicating', this will be included as an intoxicant. Unlike offences under s. 5, it is not necessary under s. 4 to show what quantity of alcohol or drug the defendant had in his or her system to convict of the offence. Answer A is therefore incorrect.

The suspicion need not be formed while the defendant is driving and can become apparent after he or she has been stopped or spoken to for some other reason (*R* v *Roff* [1976] RTR 7). Answer B is therefore incorrect.

A constable may arrest without warrant any person he or she has reasonable cause to suspect is committing an offence *or has been* committing an offence (s. 4(6)). Answer C is therefore incorrect.

Question 4

Answer **B** — Section 6(1)(c) of the Road Traffic Act 1988 states that if a constable in uniform has *reasonable cause to suspect* that a person *has been* driving a motor vehicle on a road or public place, and *has* committed an offence while the vehicle was in motion, he or she may require him or her to provide a specimen of breath.

Answer D is incorrect because the officer may require a breath sample as the driver *was* driving while committing a moving traffic offence.

Where the person is suspected of committing an offence while the vehicle was in motion, there is no requirement for the officer to suspect that he or she has alcohol in his or her body, or still has alcohol in his or her body when making the request, because of the power conferred by s. 6(1)(c) (in contrast to s. 6(1)(b) — driving/attempting/in charge with alcohol in body). Answer A is therefore incorrect.

One officer's 'reasonable cause to suspect' may arise from the observations of another officer (*Erskine* v *Hollin* [1971] RTR 199). Answer C therefore is incorrect.

Question 5

Answer **A** — It has been held that where a constable innocently fails to follow the manufacturer's instructions, it will not render the test nor any subsequent arrest unlawful (*DPP* v *Kay* [1999] RTR 109). Answer B is therefore incorrect. Answer C is also incorrect, as the arrest was not unlawful.

In addition to the case of *Kay* above, it was decided in the case of *DPP* v *Carey* [1969] 3 All ER 1662, that failing to comply with the manufacturer's instructions on the use of an approved device will mean that the person *has not provided* a preliminary breath test and *may* be asked to provide another; refusing to do so will be an offence. Answer D is incorrect, as the case is not the authority for the view that a person *must* be made to take another test. Since the purpose of the test is to indicate whether there is a *likelihood* of an offence being committed, an arrest in these circumstances is appropriate, as the test did show a positive result.

Question 6

Answer **D** — The power to conduct a breath test under s. 6(2) of the Road Traffic Act 1988 applies where an accident has occurred owing to the presence of a *motor vehicle* on a *road or public place*. Since Walsh was driving a *mechanically propelled vehicle* and not a *motor vehicle*, there is no power to request a breath test from him. Answer C is therefore incorrect. As s. 6 applies to accidents that occur in a *public place* as well as on a road, answer B is also incorrect.

There is no need for the officer making the enquiry to suspect or believe that the driver has been drinking, nor that he has committed an offence in order to require a breath test, following an accident. Answer A is therefore incorrect.

Question 7

Answer **C** — Section 6(2) of the Road Traffic Act 1988 provides that following an accident involving a motor vehicle on a road, a *constable* may require the driver to provide a specimen of breath for a breath test. The section does not require the officer to be in uniform. Answer A is therefore incorrect.

The specimen after an accident may be taken *at or near* the place where the requirement is made (answer D is therefore incorrect). If the officer making the requirement thinks fit, he or she may request that it be provided at a police station specified by that officer. There is no need for the officer to wait until he or she arrives at the station to make the requirement. Answer B is therefore incorrect.

Question 8

Answer **B** — A person who fails to provide a sample *without reasonable excuse* is guilty of an offence (s. 6(4) of the Road Traffic Act 1988). A person would have a 'reasonable excuse' if he or she was physically unable to provide a sample because to do so would entail a substantial risk to his or her health (*R v Lennard* [1973] 2 All ER 831). Clearly, where a person has a severe heart condition, as in the question, this might be a reasonable excuse.

However, this does not mean that the police can take no further action. This is merely a defence that the defendant may use to a charge of failing to provide. If the officer suspects that the person has alcohol in his or her body, he or she should not release that person to drive away! The person may be arrested in order to go through the station procedure and he or she may provide blood/urine as an alternative. Answer C is therefore incorrect. Section 6(5)(b) of the 1988 Act provides a power of arrest where a person has failed to provide a specimen *but only* if the officer has reasonable cause to suspect the driver has alcohol in his or her body. Answer A is therefore incorrect, as the power is given provisionally and therefore not every person who refuses or fails to provide a sample may be arrested.

The above provision states that the officer must suspect that the driver has *alcohol in his or her body,* in order to exercise the power of arrest. It does not state that the officer must suspect that the person is over the prescribed limit, which is why answer B is correct and answer D is incorrect.

Question 9

Answer **A** — Generally, where an officer is trespassing on a defendant's property, he or she is not entitled to require a breath test (*Fox* v *Chief Constable of Gwent* [1986] AC 281). Also, if officers are trespassing, any subsequent arrest made by them is unlawful, (*Clowser* v *Chaplin* [1981] RTR 317). However, any requirement for a sample of breath properly made and any subsequent arrest remains lawful *until* the officer becomes a trespasser.

A police officer, like any other citizen, has an implied licence to go onto certain parts of property (which might include a garden), unless and until that licence is withdrawn. It is when the licence is withdrawn that the officer may become a trespasser. Therefore, if a police officer is on the defendant's property and has not been told to leave, any requirement for a breath test and subsequent arrest is lawful, (*Pamplin* v *Fraser* [1981] RTR 494). This would still be the case even if the licence were withdrawn later. Answer D is therefore incorrect.

In the scenario given, the officer was not a trespasser until the defendant told him to leave the garden. Answer C is therefore incorrect.

Constable Dawe has no statutory power to enter the premises under s. 6(6) of the Road Traffic Act 1988, as this section only affords a power of entry following an accident involving *injury* to a person other than the driver. Answer B is incorrect as the scenario did not involve an injury.

Question 10

Answer **D** — Under s. 6(6) of the Road Traffic Act 1988, a constable may enter premises to carry out a preliminary breath test, to arrest a person following such a test and to arrest a person who has failed to supply such a test.

Before the power is used, there are *four* criteria that *must* apply. The officer must:

* *Know* that an accident has taken place, (mere suspicion is not enough).
* Have *reasonable cause to believe* that the person had been driving, attempting to drive or in charge of the vehicle (mere suspicion is not enough).
* Have *reasonable cause to suspect* that the accident involved injury to another person (here suspicion is enough).
* Have *reasonable cause to suspect* that the person he or she is seeking is in the place to be entered (again suspicion is enough).

Answer D is the only option with all the correct criteria in place and therefore answers A, B and C are incorrect.

Question 11

Answer **B** — Statement 1 is incorrect. A requirement under s. 7 of the Road Traffic Act 1988 for a breath specimen may *not* be made at any place other than a police station. Logically, a police station is the only place where such a specimen may be taken, as this is where the breath test machine is kept!

Statement 2 is correct. It was held in the case of *Pearson v Metropolitan Police Commissioner* [1988] RTR 276, that the requirement under s. 7 may be made of more than one person (in this instance three people were involved), in respect of the same vehicle, provided it is believed that one of them was driving the vehicle.

Consequently, answers A, C and D are incorrect.

Question 12

Answer **C** — For the officer to have 'reasonable cause to *believe*' that a medical reason exists, there is no need to seek medical advice first (*Dempsey v Catton* [1986] RTR 194). Answer A is therefore incorrect.

It is the objective *cause* of the belief that a medical reason exists that will be considered by the courts, not whether the officer actually did believe that a medical reason existed (*Davis* v *DPP* [1988 RTR 156). Therefore, the officer's precautionary measures were appropriate.

Practically, custody officers are often faced with this dilemma, as suspects may attempt to confuse the issue by feigning illness. Evidentially, nothing will be lost if a sample of blood is obtained, and it is often better to err on the side of caution, particularly when there is case law such as *Davis* as a fallback. Answer B is therefore incorrect.

If a person is too drunk to provide a breath specimen, that may be regarded as a 'medical reason' for requiring a sample of blood or urine (*Young* v *DPP* [1992] RTR 328). Answer D therefore is incorrect.

A note of caution should be added, as it has been the author's experience that police doctors are sometimes reluctant to take blood from a person who is very drunk, as the sample must be taken with their consent. The doctor's opinion might be that if consent is obtained from a person who does not understand what he or she is consenting to, it may be regarded as an assault.

Question 13

Answer **D** — If the machine being used at one station is unreliable, by virtue of the fact that it will not calibrate the reading correctly, it will be 'unavailable'. In this case, the driver may be taken to another station, where another machine is available, *even if the driver has already provided two samples on the inaccurate machine* (*Denny* v *DPP* [1990] RTR 417). Answer D is correct for this reason.

The prosecution may not use a breath test reading *and* a blood reading in the same case. If a requirement to provide blood/urine is made, that sample must be used and the prosecution may not revert to the evidence produced by the breath sample. In effect the blood sample replaces the breath sample (*Badkin* v *Chief Constable of South Yorkshire, The Times*, 29 August 1987). Answer A is therefore incorrect.

Answer B is incorrect as two specimens of breath must be submitted as evidence to the court. It has been held that if the defendant supplies one specimen only, this will be deemed a failure to provide.

Under s. 7(3)(b) of the Road Traffic Act 1988, the defendant *may* be asked to provide a sample of blood/urine, where the device is unavailable for breath tests. However, the case of *Denny* above shows that this is not the only option available. Answer C is therefore incorrect.

Question 14

Answer **A** — All scenarios are taken from decided cases in relation to procedure under s. 7 of the Road Traffic Act 1988, where officers have been found by the courts to have acted correctly.

In the case of *Thompson v Thynne* [1986] Crim LR 629, the court held that where an officer knew at the time that the breath test machine was unavailable due to a malfunction, he or she could require a specimen of blood/urine.

In the case of *Chief Constable of Kent v Berry* [1986] Crim LR 748, it was decided that the driver may be taken to another police station where a doctor is available.

In the case of *Chief Constable of Avon and Somerset v Kelliher* [1986] Crim LR 635 it was decided that where no trained officer was available to operate the machine, it will be 'unavailable' and a specimen of blood/urine may be requested.

Consequently, answers B, C and D are incorrect.

Question 15

Answer **C** — Where it is suspected that the driver of a vehicle, who has been requested to provide a sample under s. 7 of the Road Traffic Act 1988, is under the influence of drugs, the advice of a medical practitioner *must* be sought *before* the request is made to provide blood or urine (s. 7(3)(c)). Answers B and D are both incorrect in this respect. Answer B is also incorrect in relation to procedure, because where a person has been asked to provide a specimen of urine, there is no requirement for a medical practitioner to take the sample — it may be taken by a police officer.

When medical advice is sought in these circumstances, the doctor must give the officer a 'clear verbal' statement to the effect that the driver's condition was due to some drug, *before* the request is made for blood/urine (*Cole v DPP* [1988] RTR 224). Answer A is therefore incorrect.

Question 16

Answer **B** — The House of Lords ruling in the case of *DPP* v *Warren* [1993] AC 319 ended many arguments in relation to whether the driver should be given a preference as to whether he or she gave blood or urine. Their Lordships stated unequivocally that the decision must be made by the officer. Answer C is incorrect, as the driver will play no consultative role in the decision.

However, there will be occasions when a driver will legitimately be unable to provide a sample of blood for medical reasons. In the case of *DPP* v *Jackson; Stanley* v *DPP* [1998] 3 WLR 514, the House of Lords stressed the distinction between the role of the police officer and the doctor.

The police officer will decide *which* evidential sample should be obtained and the medical practitioner decides on the *validity of the reasons put forward by the defendant* as to why a specimen of blood should not be taken. Taking this decision a step further, the role of the officer will be to act on the 'advice' given by the doctor. Answer A is incorrect because there must be some consultation, and answer D is incorrect, as the *Stanley* case clearly shows a distinction between the decision makers — it is not a joint role.

Question 17

Answer **D** — Statement 1 is incorrect. A warning must be given when *any* specimen is required under s. 7 of the Road Traffic Act 1988 (i.e. breath, blood or urine), (s. 7(7)).

Statement 2 is also incorrect. It was held in the case of *Bobin* v *DPP* [1999] RTR 375 that as long as a warning is given to the person providing the sample, it does not matter *which* officer gives it. Therefore under s. 7(7) the warning may be given by the person requiring the sample, the custody officer or even the officer in the case. For evidential purposes, the person giving the warning should make a note that this was done.

Consequently, answers A, B and C are incorrect.

Question 18

Answer **A** — When the person has provided two samples, and the lower reading is below 50 microgrammes of alcohol in 100 millilitres of breath, the person who has provided the sample may replace the breath sample with either a specimen of blood or urine (s. 8(1) and (2) of the Road Traffic Act 1988). Although the defendant is given the choice as to whether he or she wishes to replace his or her sample, the choice as to which sample will be provided will be that of the officer. Answer C is therefore incorrect.

As with s. 7 of the 1988 Act, the possibility of medical reasons for not providing blood *must* be considered. An alleged fear of needles by the driver *is* a relevant consideration when making this decision (*DPP* v *Jackson; Stanley* v *DPP* [1998] 3 WLR 514 and also *Johnson* v *West Yorkshire Metropolitan Police* [1986] RTR 167). Answer B is therefore incorrect.

The medical advice may be given to the officer over the telephone if appropriate (*Andrews* v *DPP* [1992] RTR 1). Answer D is therefore incorrect.

Question 19

Answer **B** — Both statements are taken from decided cases in relation to s. 8 of the Road Traffic Act 1988.

Statement 1 is incorrect. When a fault occurs, which leads to a blood specimen being unsuitable, the prosecution may *not* use the original breath specimens to prove the person was over the limit (*Archbold* v *Jones* [1985] Crim LR 740).

Statement 2 is correct; a driver should be given the opportunity to state any medical reasons why blood should not be taken, but failing to give him or her that opportunity will *not* necessarily lead to the failure of the case (*DPP* v *Orchard* [2000] All ER (D) 1457). However, in practice, it is always best to err on the side of caution and provide this information as nothing is lost evidentially by doing so.

Consequently, answers A, C and D are incorrect.

Question 20

Answer **D** — Sergeant DONELLY has *not* acted correctly in these circumstances. Where a driver provides one specimen only, and fails without a reasonable excuse to provide the second sample, he or she has committed the offence of 'failing to provide' a sample (*Cracknell* v *Willis* [1987] 3 All ER 801). Answers A and C are incorrect for this reason.

'Mental impairment' may provide a reasonable excuse for failing to provide a sample. However, being drunk or under stress is not in itself enough to provide a 'reasonable excuse' for failing to provide a specimen (*DPP* v *Falzarano* [2001] RTR 14). This is confirmed by the case of *DPP* v *Beech* [1992] Crim LR 64, where it was decided that where the defendant's mental capacity to understand the warning was impaired by his or her drunkenness, this was not a 'reasonable' excuse. Answer B is therefore incorrect.

Question 21

Answer **D** — What amounts to a 'reasonable excuse' is a matter of law. However, it has been left for the courts to decide whether or not a defendant *had* a reasonable excuse, having regard to the circumstances in each case. There is a long list in *Blackstone's Road Traffic Manual* identifying what will *not* amount to a 'reasonable excuse'. There are few examples of what *will* amount to a 'reasonable excuse' and these centre around physical and mental incapacity and the ability to understand because of *non*-self-induced matters (i.e. language barriers).

Scenario 2 is the only option out of the four where a person might be said to have a reasonable excuse. It would seem that this particular problem could be avoided under s. 7 of the Road Traffic Act 1988, if the Codes of Practice under Police and Criminal Evidence Act 1984, in relation to detention of persons in custody, are followed. The need for an interpreter should have been identified *before* the station procedure was carried out (this might be different in relation to roadside breath tests of course!).

Scenarios 1, 3 and 4 have been held *not* to be 'reasonable excuses'. It has been the author's experience that many 'delaying tactics' are used in respect of specimens and scenarios 3 and 4 are not uncommon. In practice, if the custody officer has time, and there is one readily available, allowing a person to speak to his or her solicitor can often be a worthwhile exercise, so long as the process is not held up for an unreasonable time. (Allowing the defendant to read the Codes of Practice may take a little longer!)

Consequently, answers A, B and C are incorrect.

Question 22

Answer **C** — Both scenarios are taken from decided cases and are both examples of failing to provide specimens without a 'reasonable excuse'.

Scenario 1 reinforces the fact that consent may not be accompanied by 'conditions' laid down by the defendant. In *Rushton* v *Higgins* [1972] Crim LR 440, it was decided that once consent is given to provide a sample of blood, it is for the doctor to say from which part of the body it will be taken. Any insistence on a different course of action will be a refusal.

In relation to scenario 2, samples of urine will be admissible as long as they are provided within the time set out under s. 7(5) of the Road Traffic Act 1988 and that there are two distinct samples (as opposed to two samples taken during the same act of urinating) (*Prosser* v *Dickeson* [1982] RTR 96).

Consequently, answers A, B and D are incorrect.

Question 23

Answer **B** — Under s. 15(2) of the Road Traffic Offenders Act 1988, the court *must* take into account any evidence of the proportion of alcohol or drugs in any specimen supplied by the accused.

Section 15(2) goes on to say that the court *must* assume that the proportion of *alcohol* in the accused's body at the time of the alleged offence was *not less* that the specimen provided (in other words at least the same). This assumption *does not* apply in cases where the defendant is alleged to have taken drugs. Answer B is correct for this reason.

Section 15(3) states that the accused may introduce evidence that he or she had consumed alcohol between the alleged driving offence and the provision of the specimen and that if he or she had not done so, the proportion of *alcohol* in his or her sample would not have exceeded the prescribed limit. Answer D is incorrect as this evidence *is* introduced by the *defence*.

However, as subsection (3) applies to the introduction of such evidence in cases involving *alcohol* only, it would not be applicable in the circumstances outlined. As this will not affect the ruling that the court must *take evidence into account* of the sample provided, answer A is incorrect.

This section applies to offences under s. 3A, 4 or 5 of the Road Traffic Act 1988. Millard is accused of an offence under s. 3A and therefore answer C is incorrect.

Question 24

Answer **B** — The question deals with three elements of the provision of samples to the defendant: providing a sample on request and the timing of when the sample is divided and actually given to the defendant. Only answer B contains the correct statements for all three elements. The other answers contain a mixture of correct and incorrect statements. The correct statements are shown below.

Section 15(5) of the Road Traffic Offenders Act 1988 states that it must be shown that the defendant was supplied with a specimen *if he or she asked for one.*

Although the specimen must be divided 'at the time', there is no need for it to be done in the defendant's presence (*DPP* v *Elstob* [1992] RTR 45).

Although the specimen must be divided at the time, there is no need to provide the defendant with his or her part 'at the time'. This may be done within a 'reasonable time' thereafter (*R* v *Sharp* [1968] 2 QB 564).

Consequently, answers A, C and D are incorrect.

Question 25

Answer **A** — Statement 1 is correct. Under s. 15(4) of the Road Traffic Act 1988 the prosecution must prove beyond reasonable doubt that the defendant consented to supplying a specimen of blood (*Friel* v *Dickinson* [1992] RTR 366). This may be proved by documentary evidence signed by a medical practitioner (s. 16(2)).

Statement 2 is incorrect. It is correct that the defendant must be provided with a copy of any statement produced by the breath test machine. However, it has been held that there is no requirement for the *copy* to be signed by a police officer (*Chief Constable of Surrey* v *Wickens* [1985] RTR 277).

Consequently, answers B, C and D are incorrect.

Question 26

Answer **D** — Section 10 of the Road Traffic Act 1988 allows for the detention of a person who has provided a specimen of breath, blood or urine, until it appears to a constable that were the person to drive a mechanically propelled vehicle on a road, he or she would not be committing an offence. The power does not apply if it appears to a constable that there is no likelihood of the person driving such a vehicle on a road. There is no mention of a person having been charged or reported for an offence, merely that they have been required to provide the relevant sample. Answer C is therefore incorrect.

Under s. 10(3), a constable *must* consult a medical practitioner on *any question arising under this section whether a person's ability to drive properly is or might be impaired through drugs.* The constable *must* act on such advice. This is mandatory; therefore both answers A and B are incorrect.

Question 27

Answer **B** — Under s. 9 of the Road Traffic Act 1988, when a person is in hospital, he or she shall not be *required* to provide a specimen of breath, or laboratory test, unless the medical practitioner in *immediate charge of his/her case* has been notified and approves. The officer *may not* even make the requirement unless the doctor approves. Answers A and D are therefore incorrect.

The doctor that may give approval shall be the doctor in immediate charge of the patient (not simply any doctor in the hospital). Answer A is also incorrect for this reason.

Answer C is incorrect as a requirement may be made in the above circumstances.

Question 28

Answer **B** — A specimen of blood may be taken under s. 9 of the Road Traffic Act 1988, from a patient at a hospital, provided the doctor in immediate charge of his or her case agrees. Section 9 applies to both breath samples and samples of blood.

However, if a patient provides a positive reading or fails to provide a sample at a hospital, he or she cannot be arrested while still a 'patient' (s. 6(5)). Answer B is therefore correct and answer C is incorrect as, even though the officer sought permission to take the second sample, the arrest that preceded it was unlawful.

Since the arrest was unlawful, answer A is incorrect, as the patient should not have been taken to a police station in these circumstances. However, if the person had been arrested *after* ceasing to be a patient, she could have been taken to the station to provide a sample (see *Webber* v *DPP* [1998] RTR 111).

Answer D is incorrect as permission must be sought from a doctor for *each* sample that is required under s. 9(1).

6 INSURANCE

STUDY PREPARATION

Insurance matters are straightforward and, after the detail of the previous chapter, are also relatively brief.

It is important to understand the requirements for compulsory insurance and the main related offences — including causing and permitting.

The duties on drivers and owners in relation to production of insurance documents are also important when studying this area.

QUESTIONS

Question 1

NEWBURY persuaded DAVIS to lend him his car to take his mother shopping. DAVIS agreed to do so, but on condition that NEWBURY arranged his own insurance. While driving DAVIS's car, NEWBURY was involved in an accident and it was discovered that he had no insurance and that DAVIS's insurance did not cover him to drive either.

Would DAVIS be guilty of 'permitting' an offence by NEWBURY of driving without insurance?

[A] Yes, because permitting without insurance is an offence of absolute liability.

[B] No, because he told NEWBURY to insure the car before driving it, and has therefore discharged any liability for this offence.

[C] Yes, because even though he told NEWBURY to insure the car, he should have seen evidence that he had done so.

[D] No, because permitting without insurance is not an offence of absolute liability.

Question 2

In relation to an employee using a vehicle on a road without insurance, which of the following statements, if either, is/are true?

1. The driver's statement that he or she was using the vehicle in the course of employment will be sufficient in itself to convict the owner of the offence of 'permitting'.

2. If a driver alleges that he or she was using a vehicle during the course of employment and was not aware it was uninsured, the burden of proof lies with him or her and the case will be judged on the balance of probabilities.

[A] Statement 1 only.

[B] Statement 2 only.

[C] Both statements.

[D] Neither statement.

Question 3

BROWN was involved in an accident while driving his employer's delivery van. The accident occurred about two miles from his normal delivery route. At the time, BROWN was helping a friend by giving him a lift. The insurance policy for the van allows its use in connection with business only and it is company policy not to carry passengers in vehicles. BROWN does not have an insurance policy of his own and the journey was not authorised by his company.

Would the insurance policy for the van cover BROWN's use of the vehicle at the time of the accident?

[A] Yes, BROWN's use of the vehicle would be covered in these circumstances.
[B] No, because the van was being used in a manner not authorised by BROWN's employer.
[C] No, as BROWN has made a detour from his normal route, his use of the vehicle would not be covered.
[D] No, as the van was not being used for business purposes at the time.

Question 4

Under s. 144 of the Road Traffic Act 1988, certain vehicles are exempt from the requirement for insurance.

Which of the following vehicles are **not** covered by the exemption?

1. A vehicle owned by the National Criminal Intelligence Service.
2. A motor vehicle being towed by another vehicle.
3. A vehicle owned by an off-duty police officer being used for police purposes.

[A] Vehicle 2 only.
[B] Vehicles 1 and 3 only.
[C] All of the above.
[D] Vehicles 2 and 3 only.

Question 5

Section 165 of the Road Traffic Act 1988 provides the authority for a constable to require the production of a certificate of insurance from the driver of a motor vehicle on a road or public place.

Following such a requirement, who may produce the certificate?

[A] Only the person who was driving the vehicle at the time the requirement was made.

[B] Only the person who was the owner of the vehicle at the time the requirement was made.

[C] Any person nominated by the person of whom the request is made.

[D] Any person nominated by the person of whom the request is made, provided they were nominated at the time the request was made.

Question 6

STINTON had broken his arm and asked his friend FLEMING to drive him to the pub. On their way there, FLEMING was involved in an accident, and STINTON further damaged his broken arm. It was discovered that FLEMING was not insured to drive the vehicle. STINTON had to give up work because of the long-term damage to his arm, and made a claim for compensation to the Motor Insurers' Bureau for damages.

Is STINTON's claim likely to succeed in these circumstances?

[A] No, as passengers in the offending vehicle are not entitled to claim.

[B] Yes, as he was not involved in a criminal act at the time of the accident.

[C] No, as he was a passenger who was *using* the vehicle at the time.

[D] Yes, as the driver of the vehicle is known and was uninsured.

ANSWERS

Question 1

Answer **B** — Permitting the use of a vehicle by another without insurance is an offence under s. 143 of the Road Traffic Act 1988, and generally the offence is one of absolute liability. Answer D is therefore incorrect.

If, however, a person allows another to use his or her vehicle on the express condition that the other person insures it first, the lender cannot be guilty of 'permitting' (*Newbury* v *Davis* [1974] RTR 367). There is no mention of having to check the person's certificate before allowing them to drive and presumably stating the condition will suffice. Answers A and C are therefore incorrect.

Question 2

Answer **B** — Statement 1 is incorrect. Where an owner is suspected of committing an offence of 'permitting' without insurance, the burden of proof lies with the prosecution to show the driver *was* acting in the course of his or her employment. The driver's statement that he or she was doing so will *not* in itself be sufficient to convict the owner of the offence of 'permitting' (*Jones* v *DPP* [1999] RTR 1).

Statement 2 is correct. Section 143(3) of the Road Traffic Act 1988 provides a defence for an employee, if he or she is using the employer's vehicle without insurance, provided he or she was not the owner of the vehicle, it was used in the course of his or her employment and he or she did not know or have any reason to believe that the vehicle was not insured. The burden of proof lies with the employee and the issue will be judged on the balance of probabilities.

Consequently, answers A, C and D are incorrect.

Question 3

Answer **A** — A vehicle may be insured for 'business purposes' and normally, if an employee deviates from the ordinary course of his or her duties, the policy will be invalidated. However, it was decided in the case of *Ballance* v *Brown* [1955] Crim LR 384 that taking a two-mile detour to give someone a lift will not necessarily invalidate the employer's insurance. Answers C and D are therefore incorrect.

In a further case that emphasises this point, *Marsh* v *Moores* [1949] 2 All ER 27, it was held that an employee driving an employer's vehicle in an unauthorised manner will not negate the effect of the insurance policy. Answer B is therefore incorrect.

Question 4

Answer **A** — Statements 1 and 3 are correct. Among the vehicles listed as exempt from requiring insurance are:

- Crown vehicles while being used as such (see the Scottish case of *Salt* v *MacKnight* 1947 SC (J) 99);
- police authority vehicles and vehicles being used for police purposes — which includes a vehicle owned by an off-duty police officer being used for police purposes (*Jones* v *Chief Constable of Bedfordshire* [1987] RTR 332);
- a vehicle owned by the National Criminal Intelligence Service or the National Crime Squad (s. 144(2)(ba) Road Traffic Act 1988).

Statement 2 is incorrect. A motor vehicle being towed by another vehicle will still be a 'motor vehicle', which means that it will still require insurance when used on a road (*Milstead* v *Sexton* [1964] Crim LR 474).

Consequently, answers B, C and D are incorrect.

Question 5

Answer **C** — The certificate need not be produced in person, which means that the person who was driving the vehicle may elect another person to produce it for him or her. Answer A is therefore incorrect.

It is *not* necessary to 'nominate' the person at the time the request is made to produce the documents. Answer D is therefore incorrect.

Answer B is incorrect as the driver may at times be different from the owner; therefore the power exists in relation to the driver (unless of course the owner is suspected of using, causing or permitting, in which case he or she may be asked to produce under s. 165(1)(c) of the Road Traffic Act 1988).

Question 6

Answer **C** — The purpose of the Motor Insurers' Bureau (MIB) is to provide compensation where someone is unable to pursue a valid claim against another following a road traffic accident, i.e. because the other party is not insured, not known or traceable or insured by a company now in liquidation.

Where a person other than the driver is injured, it will be a road traffic accident. Such a person may make a claim (provided he or she does not fall within the categories listed below). Answer A is therefore incorrect.

The MIB will *not* compensate those who are involved in deliberate criminal acts, nor will it pursue a claim on behalf of a person who was 'using' a vehicle at a time he or she was a passenger. As the owner of the vehicle in the scenario was in it, and it was being used for his purpose, he was 'using' it without insurance and therefore cannot make a claim. Answers B and D are therefore incorrect.

7 SAFETY MEASURES

STUDY PREPARATION

Safety measures cover a range of statutory provisions, including the requirements for seat belts, crash helmets and speed restrictions.

Once again this is a pretty straightforward area.

QUESTIONS

Question 1

CLEMENT was driving on a road in his car. CLEMENT's daughter, JUDY, aged 13, was sitting in the back. CLEMENT was wearing a safety belt, but JUDY was not. The car was old, and was not fitted with safety belts to the rear. The front passenger seat was occupied by CLEMENT's son BARRY, aged 16. BARRY was wearing a safety belt.

Have any of the people in the car committed an offence in relation to JUDY's failure to wear a safety belt?

[A]   Yes, CLEMENT only, because of JUDY's age.
[B]   Yes, JUDY only because of her age.
[C]   Yes, CLEMENT only, he should have moved JUDY to the front seat.
[D]   No, neither has committed an offence in these circumstances.

Question 2

KRAUSER, aged 25 has a full licence to ride a motor cycle and one day, he gave his brother PAUL, aged 15, a ride on the road as a pillion passenger on the motorcycle. They were stopped by Constable FRY, because PAUL was not wearing a crash helmet. At the time, the motor cycle had a side car attached to it.

Who, if either, would commit an offence in these circumstances (because of PAUL's failure to wear a helmet)?

[A]   Neither, as the motorcycle was fitted with a sidecar.
[B]   Both, because of PAUL's age.
[C]   KRAUSER only, because of PAUL's age.
[D]   PAUL only, because of his age.

Question 3

Under the Transport Act 2000, certain roads may be designated as 'quiet lanes' or 'home zones'. Who is provided with the power to designate such roads?

[A]   The local authority.
[B]   The Secretary of State.
[C]   The local Chief of Police.
[D]   The Highways Authority.

Question 4

HARVEY was driving in a car at 40 mph along a road, when he was stopped by Constable UNDERWOOD. The officer believed that HARVEY was speeding, as the road was a 'restricted road'.

What physical features must be apparent to the officer to identify the road as a 'restricted road'?

[A]   Street lamps less than 200 yards apart and signs signifying the 30 mph speed limit.

[B]   Street lamps not less than 200 yards apart or signs signifying the 30 mph speed limit.

[C]   Street lamps not more than 200 yards apart or signs signifying the 30 mph speed limit.

[D]   Street lamps not more than than 200 metres apart or signs signifying the 30 mph speed limit.

Question 5

Which of the following statements, if either, is/are true in relation to 'temporary speed limits'?

1.   A temporary speed restriction placed by a traffic authority may not exceed 18 months' duration without approval from the Secretary of State.
2.   Where a person contravenes a temporary speed restriction, corroboration is not required, but a notice of intended prosecution is.

[A]   Statement 1 only
[B]   Statement 2 only.
[C]   Both statements.
[D]   Neither statement.

Question 6

Constable WOODS and Constable HUSSEIN were on duty in a marked police vehicle. They were driving along a restricted road, which had a speed limit of 30 mph. They followed DICKSON, who was driving at 40 mph in his car, for about a mile. The officers stopped DICKSON and spoke to him.

Would the officers be able to give evidence of DICKSON's speed, in order to prosecute him for the offence of speeding?

[A] No, their evidence does not amount to corroboration, and would not be accepted in court.

[B] Yes, provided it can be shown that they saw the vehicle at exactly the same time.

[C] Yes, the evidence that they both saw the vehicle speeding is sufficient alone to prosecute.

[D] Yes, corroboration is not required, as the offence took place in a restricted road.

Question 7

In which of the following scenarios, if any, will an offence have been committed under the motorway regulations?

1. DUVALL rode a motor cycle with an engine/cylinder capacity of 99cc on the motorway. He has passed his motorcycle test.

2. PASK held a full driving licence to drive a car, but was learning to drive a large goods vehicle. She drove the goods vehicle on the motorway.

3. FLETCHER was towing a caravan on the motorway and used the outside lane to overtake a vehicle.

[A] All of the above.

[B] Scenario 3 only.

[C] Scenarios 1 and 2 only.

[D] Scenarios 2 and 3 only.

ANSWERS

Question 1

Answer **D** — If the person failing to wear a safety belt is under 14, the driver of the vehicle is responsible and commits an offence (s. 15 of the Road Traffic Act 1988). If the person failing to wear the safety belt is over 14, he or she is responsible for his or her own actions and commits the offence (s. 14 of the Road Traffic Act 1988). If an offence had been committed in this scenario, Clement would have been responsible. Answer A is therefore incorrect.

However, there is an exemption to the offence if there is no seat belt 'available' for passengers. Further, if all the seats are properly occupied there is no requirement to move a child from one part of the vehicle where no belts are fitted, to another part where they are. Since no offences were committed, answers A, B and C are incorrect.

An offence would have been committed if Judy had been under 12 and less than 150 cms in height. In those circumstances, she would have to sit in the front of the vehicle.

Question 2

Answer **B** — Section 16(1) of the Road Traffic Act 1988 makes it an offence to ride on a motorcycle without a crash helmet. 'Ride on' includes being a pillion passenger.

If the pillion passenger is *under 16*, the offence is committed by *both the rider and the passenger*. If the pillion passenger is *16 or over*, he or she is responsible alone. This is in contrast to seat belt legislation, where young passengers *are not* responsible for their own actions. As the person in the question was 15, both he and the driver commit the offence. Answers C and D are therefore incorrect.

A motor cycle with a sidecar attached will still be a *motor bicycle* for the purposes of the section and the offence is committed. Answer A is therefore incorrect. If the passenger had been sitting in the sidecar, he *would* have been exempt from having to wear a crash helmet (s. 16(1)).

Question 3

Answer **A** — Under the Transport Act 2000, certain roads may be designated as 'quiet lanes' or 'home zones' by *local authorities*. Consequently, answers B, C and D are incorrect.

Question 4

Answer **C** — Under s. 82(1)(a) of the Road Traffic Regulation Act 1984, a 'restricted road' is one which has a system of street lamps *not more than 200 yards apart*. This is the minimum requirement, and these features will mean that 30 mph signs are not required (s. 85(5)). Answer A is therefore incorrect.

The street lamps must be *200 yards apart, or less*. Therefore answers B and D are incorrect.

If a road does not have such street lamps, it must have traffic signs stating the speed limit (s. 85(4)). Conversely, a road with street lamps of less than 200 yards apart may have a higher speed limit than 30 mph, but there must be signs indicating the limit.

The speed limit for a 'restricted road' is 30 mph, and it is an offence to drive a motor vehicle on a road exceeding this limit (s. 81(1)).

Question 5

Answer **A** — Statement 1 is correct, a temporary speed restriction placed by a traffic authority *may not* exceed 18 months' duration without approval from the Secretary of State.

Statement 2 is incorrect, where a person contravenes a temporary speed restriction, corroboration is *not* required. A notice of intended prosecution is also *not* required.

Consequently, answers B, C and D are incorrect.

Question 6

Answer **B** — Under s. 89(2) of the Road Traffic Regulation Act 1984, a person may not be convicted solely on the evidence of one person for exceeding the speed limit. In other words, corroboration is required (unless the offence took place on a motorway). Corroboration is required when the offence takes place on a restricted road. Answer D is therefore incorrect.

Corroboration is normally provided by equipment in a police vehicle, however, two police officers *may* provide sufficient evidence in a case of speeding, but the court will decide how much weight to give to such evidence. It is important to show that the officers saw the vehicle at *exactly* the same time (*Brighty* v *Pearson* [1938] 4 All ER 127). Answers A and C are incorrect for this reason.

Question 7

Answer **B** — The Motorways Traffic (England and Wales) Regulations 1982 (SI 1982 No. 1163) stipulate which vehicles may use the motorways, and *how* they may be used:

- A motor cycle with an engine/cylinder capacity of less than *50cc* is not allowed on the motorway.
- A learner driver may not use the motorway. However, a person who holds an ordinary licence may drive a LGV or a PCV and may do so on the motorway even if they are learning to drive those particular classes of vehicles.
- Regulation 12 lists vehicles which are prohibited from using the outside lane of a motorway. Vehicles drawing trailers are listed; a caravan is a trailer. Also listed are LGV's exceeding 7.5 tonnes and PCV's over 12m long.

Consequently, an offence has been committed under scenario 3 only and therefore answers A, C and D are incorrect.

8   OTHER MEASURES AFFECTING SAFETY

STUDY PREPARATION

The areas covered by this chapter are wide and varied, ranging from the disposal of abandoned vehicles to powers under the Terrorism Act 2000.

Many of the police powers covered are particularly useful in practical situations and therefore will be of interest to those who train and test police officers.

QUESTIONS

Question 1

MILLS placed a handcart, in a busy shopping precinct, in order to sell Christmas decorations. The stall was situated in a street, which was open to pedestrians only and where no vehicles were allowed. Constable CHADD was passing and asked MILLS to remove the handcart, as she believed it was causing an obstruction.

Under what circumstances, if at all, may Constable CHADD arrest MILLS for obstruction?

[A] None, as MILLS was not in charge of a motor vehicle or trailer.
[B] Only if MILLS refuses to remove the obstruction on request.
[C] None, as MILLS is not obstructing a road.
[D] Only if the general arrest conditions under s. 25 of the Police and Criminal Evidence Act 1984 are satisfied.

Question 2

The Terrorism Act 2000 provides the police with powers to place restrictions on parking, to prevent acts of terrorism.

In relation to this power, who may authorise such restrictions, and for how long?

[A] A Superintendent, for a period not exceeding 28 days.
[B] An Assistant Chief Constable/Commander, for a period not exceeding 21 days.
[C] An Assistant Chief Constable/Commander, for a period not exceeding 28 days.
[D] A Chief Officer of Police/Commander, for a period not exceeding 28 days.

Question 3

PAINES lives on a main road, on a sharp bend. PAINES owns a caravan, which he keeps on his drive. He returned from holiday one evening and went to bed, forgetting to place blocks under the caravan's wheels to prevent it from moving. During the night, PAINES' caravan rolled down the drive and into the middle of the road, causing a danger to passing motorists.

Has PAINES committed an offence under s. 22A of the Road Traffic Act 1988 (causing danger to other road users)?

[A] No, as he did not intend to create a danger for road users.
[B] Yes, as he was reckless as to whether danger would be caused to road users.
[C] No, the offence may only be committed when a person interferes with equipment in the road.
[D] No, provided no injury or damage was caused by the caravan's presence.

Question 4

GRANT bought some fireworks and one evening, he discharged some rockets while standing on the pavement outside his house.

Has GRANT committed an offence by discharging the fireworks in these circumstances?

[A] No, as the fireworks were not discharged in the road.
[B] Yes, provided a danger was caused to people using the road.
[C] Yes, provided people using the road were injured, interrupted or endangered.
[D] Yes, the offence is committed by simply discharging the firework.

Question 5

AHMED used a 3.5 tonne van to deliver furniture. AHMED was delivering to a house situated in a street, which had a grass verge in the centre of the road, dividing two carriageways. There were no parking spaces outside the delivery address; therefore, AHMED parked the vehicle on the grass verge until a space became available.

Has AHMED committed an offence contrary to s. 19 of the Road Traffic Act 1988, (parking commercial vehicles on verges)?

[A]   No, because of the vehicle's weight.
[B]   Yes, as the vehicle was parked on land in the centre of the road.
[C]   Yes, provided the vehicle was causing a danger.
[D]   No, as the vehicle was not parked on a verge at the side of a road.

Question 6

Section 22 of the Road Traffic Act 1988 provides an offence of leaving a vehicle in a position, or condition, or in circumstances as to involve danger of injury.

In relation to when an offence may be committed under this section, which of the following statements is correct?

It may be committed by:

[A]   A vehicle or a trailer, but only when stationary.
[B]   A vehicle only, when stationary.
[C]   A vehicle or trailer, when stationary or moving.
[D]   A vehicle only, when stationary or moving.

Question 7

Which of the following statements, if either, is/are correct in relation to the issue of 'orange badges', under the Chronically Sick and Disabled Persons Act 1970?

1. The scheme only applies to offences under the Road Traffic Regulation Act 1984.
2. A local authority may require the return of a badge, where a person has misused it in a way which has led to at least two convictions.

[A] Statement 1 only.
[B] Statement 2 only.
[C] Both statements.
[D] Neither statement.

Question 8

HARRIS was drunk one evening, walking along the street. He was seen by Constable ADDIS to climb onto the bonnet of a car and run over the roof, jumping off the vehicle from the boot. He did this to several vehicles in the street.

Would Constable ADDIS be able to arrest HARRIS for tampering with vehicles in these circumstances?

[A] No, HARRIS has not interfered with the brakes or other mechanism of the vehicles therefore he had not committed the offence.
[B] Yes, HARRIS has committed the offence, for which he may be arrested.
[C] No, HARRIS has committed the offence of 'getting on to vehicles', which is a summary offence.
[D] No, HARRIS is guilty of tampering with a vehicle, but there is no power of arrest.

Question 9

DOUGLAS lived near some woodland, which was accessible from the road. One day, he drove to the woodland in his van and abandoned a settee and two chairs in a clearing in the woods.

Has DOUGLAS committed an offence under the Refuse Disposal (Amenity) Act 1978 (disposing property on land)?

[A]   No, the offence relates to abandoning a motor vehicle only.
[B]   Yes, he has committed an offence in these circumstances.
[C]   No, he has not abandoned anything on a highway or land forming part of a highway.
[D]   No, the offence relates to abandoning a motor vehicle or part of a motor vehicle only.

Question 10

A cycle race was due to take place in a town centre on a Sunday. CAREY had parked a caravan on the road the night before, intending to sell burgers from it to spectators the next day. CAREY had left the caravan on double yellow lines and it was in a street which formed part of the route for the race. Constable SHEEHY was sent to the scene to arrange for its removal before the start of the race.

Did Constable SHEEHY have the authority to remove the vehicle in these circumstances?

[A]   Yes, she had the authority to remove the vehicle herself or arrange its removal.
[B]   No, she would have to arrange for CAREY to remove it.
[C]   No, the vehicle was not causing an actual obstruction to people using the road.
[D]   No, the power to remove vehicles applies to motor vehicles only.

Question 11

PETERS owned a trials motor cycle, which was not intended for use on roads. Near PETERS' house is an area of common land and he took his motor cycle there one day. PETERS had just started up his motor cycle and had ridden onto the land, approximately 10 yards from the road, when he was stopped by Constable MENDEZ.

Has PETERS committed an offence of driving on land other than a road, in these circumstances?

[A] No, as he was not driving a motor vehicle.
[B] Yes, as he has driven on common land other than a road.
[C] No, he has driven within 15 yards of the road.
[D] Yes, as he has driven on common land within 15 yards of the road.

Question 12

SHAH has hired PRICE to do some building work at his house. PRICE has hired a skip from BARRY for a period of three weeks. After a week, neighbours complain to the police that the skip is unlit during the night and is causing a danger to motorists.

Who has committed an offence in relation to the skip in these circumstances?

[A] SHAH only.
[B] PRICE only.
[C] PRICE and BARRY only.
[D] BARRY only.

Question 13

In relation to pedestrian crossings under the Regulations made under the Road Traffic Regulation Act 1984, which of the following statements, if either, is/are correct?

1. Failure by a driver to stop at a crossing in contravention of the Regulations is an absolute offence.
2. Failure by a driver to observe crossing Regulations will provide sufficient proof that a person has driven without due care and attention.

[A] Statement 1 only.
[B] Statement 2 only.
[C] Both statements.
[D] Neither statement.

Question 14

TROTT was working as a school crossing patrol outside a school at 7.50 am. BOYCE was riding on the road on his pedal cycle, when TROTT stood in the road to allow some people to cross. As none of the people were school children, BOYCE did not stop his cycle. TROTT was wearing her uniform and exhibiting her sign at the time of the incident.

Has BOYCE committed an offence in these circumstances?

[A] No, because of the time of day.
[B] Yes, an offence has been committed.
[C] No, because the people crossing were not children.
[D] No, because he was not driving a motor vehicle.

ANSWERS

Question 1

Answer **D** — The offence may either be committed under s. 137 of the Highways Act 1980, reg. 103 of the Road Vehicles (Construction and Use) Regulations 1986 (SI 1986 No. 1078) or s. 28 of the Town Police Clauses Act 1847 (outside London). A power of arrest is provided for an offence committed under the Highways Act 1980 only, provided the general arrest conditions under s. 25 of the Police and Criminal Evidence Act 1984 are satisfied. Answer B is therefore incorrect.

The offence under the Highways Act 1980 requires a person to *wilfully obstruct the free passage along a highway*. There is no requirement that the person is using or in charge of a motor vehicle or trailer to commit an offence under this Act. Answer A is therefore incorrect.

A 'highway' is a way over which the public has a right to pass and re-pass by foot, horse or vehicle (*Lang* v *Hindhaugh* [1986] RTR 271). The offence may be committed on a highway under the Highways Act 1980. Answer C is therefore incorrect.

Question 2

Answer **C** — The power under the Terrorism Act 2000 is given to any officer of or above the rank of Assistant Chief Constable/Commander. Where it appears expedient to such a person to do so, he or she may authorise the imposition of prohibitions or restrictions on parking in a specified area for a period not exceeding 28 days. Answer C is therefore the only possible correct answer and answers A, B and D are incorrect.

Question 3

Answer **A** — The offence is committed under s. 22A of the Road Traffic Act 1988, when a person *intentionally and without lawful authority or reasonable excuse* causes anything to be on or over the road in such circumstances that it would be obvious to a reasonable person that to do so would be dangerous.

Although Paines could be said to have been the cause of the danger, he did not *intend* the act to happen. The offence is *not* committed when a person is merely reckless. Answer B is therefore incorrect.

Under s. 22A the offender must intend to cause anything to be in a road, *or* intend to interfere with anything. The offence may be committed if either of those situations is present. There is no need to show that the person *intends* to create danger. Answer C is therefore incorrect.

There is no requirement to prove that a person was injured or property was damaged; it is the potential danger that matters. Answer D is therefore incorrect.

Question 4

Answer **C** — Under s. 161 of the Highways Act 1980, a person commits an offence if he or she discharges any firearm or firework within 15.24 metres (50 feet) of the centre of the highway, and in consequence a user of the highway is injured, interrupted or endangered.

As the offence took place on the pavement, which would be 50 feet from the centre of the highway, answer A is incorrect.

Answer B is incorrect as a user of the highway must be injured, interrupted *or* endangered.

Answer D is incorrect as there must be a consequence, i.e. an injury, interruption or danger must occur as a result of the discharged firework.

Question 5

Answer **A** — Under s. 19 of the Road Traffic Act 1988, an offence is committed by a *heavy* commercial vehicle, which is parked wholly or in part on the verge of a road, or any land situated between two carriageways that is not a footway, or on a footway. Answer D is incorrect as the offence may be committed in the middle of the road also.

Answer B is incorrect as the vehicle was not a heavy commercial vehicle, i.e. one which exceeded 7.5 tonnes.

There is no requirement to prove that any danger was caused by the vehicle's presence. Answer C is therefore incorrect.

Question 6

Answer **C** — An offence may be committed under s. 22 of the Road Traffic Act 1988 by a vehicle or a trailer drawn by it. Answers B and D are therefore incorrect.

The offence may be committed either by a stationary vehicle *or* by a moving vehicle, when the offence is connected with the conditions or circumstances (*Maguire* v *Crouch* (1940) 104 JP 445). Answer A is therefore incorrect.

Answer C is the only option which combines the answers correctly.

Question 7

Answer **A** — Statement 1 is correct; the scheme will only apply to offences under the Road Traffic Regulation Act 1984.

Statement 2 is incorrect; a local authority may refuse to issue a badge, or require the return of a badge, where a person has misused it in a way which has led to at least *three* convictions.

Consequently, answers B, C and D are incorrect.

Question 8

Answer **D** — Under s. 25 of the Road Traffic Act 1988, a person commits an offence if he or she *gets on to a vehicle* or tampers with the brake or mechanism of a vehicle or trailer which is parked in the road or in a local authority car park. Answer A is therefore incorrect.

There is a specific offence under s. 26 of the Act of getting on to a vehicle. However, this offence may be committed only where a person gets onto a vehicle in motion. Answer C is therefore incorrect.

The offence of tampering with a vehicle is a *summary* offence, with no specific power of arrest. Answer B is therefore incorrect.

Question 9

Answer **B** — An offence may be committed under s. 2 of the Refuse Disposal (Amenity) Act 1978 either by abandoning a motor vehicle or anything which formed part of a motor vehicle (s. 2(1)(a)), *or* by abandoning any thing *other than a motor vehicle* (s. 2(1)(b)). Answers A and D are therefore incorrect.

The offence is complete when property as referred to above, is abandoned *either* on any land forming part of the highway, *or* on any land in the open air. Presumably this would include private property, if it is in the open air. Answer C is therefore incorrect.

Question 10

Answer **A** — Under the Removal and Disposal of Vehicles Regulations 1986 (SI 1986 No. 183), a constable may require the owner of a vehicle to remove it (reg. 3). To implement the removal of a vehicle under reg. 3, it must be broken down, causing a danger or obstruction, or committing an offence such as a parking offence.

Under reg. 4, a constable may remove a vehicle himself/herself, or arrange its removal. In these circumstances, a vehicle must have broken down, or have been abandoned without lawful authority.

In the circumstances of the question, the officer could arrange for the removal of the vehicle without contacting the owner, as the vehicle is on yellow lines without lawful authority. Answers B and C are therefore incorrect.

The 1986 Regulations are not restricted to 'motor' vehicles, and therefore a caravan will be a trailer, which in turn will be a vehicle. Answer D is therefore incorrect.

Question 11

Answer **B** — Under s. 34 of the Road Traffic Act 1988, a person commits an offence who drives a *mechanically propelled vehicle* on any common land, moorland or land of any other description, not being part of a road.

The offence has been reworded by the Countryside and Rights of Way Act 2000, which extended the offence to include 'mechanically propelled' vehicles, rather than 'motor vehicles'. Answer A is therefore incorrect.

As soon as the person drives on the land, he or she commits the offence. Answer D is therefore incorrect.

A defence is provided for a person who has driven onto the land within 15 yards of the road *in order to park the vehicle*. There is no general defence of driving within 15 yards of the road only. Answer C is therefore incorrect.

Question 12

Answer **D** — Under s. 139(4)(a) of the Highways Act 1980, a skip which has been deposited on a road must be 'properly lighted' during the hours of darkness. Section 139(4) states that the *owner* of the skip will be responsible for ensuring that it complies with the conditions imposed under the Act. Answer A is therefore incorrect.

Section 139(11) of the Act states that if a skip is either hired, or made subject of a hire purchase agreement for *not less than one month*, the person *in possession* of it will become the 'owner'. Since the builder in the scenario hired it for three weeks, which *is* less than a month, the actual owner, Barry, retains responsibility for it. Answers B and C are therefore incorrect.

Question 13

Answer **A** — Statement 1 is correct; the failure by a driver to stop at a crossing in contravention of the Regulations made under the Road Traffic Regulation Act 1984 is an absolute offence. There is no need to show any particular state of mind by the driver.

Statement 2 is incorrect; the failure by a driver to observe the crossing Regulations will *not* in itself provide sufficient proof that a person has driven without due care and attention. Further proof would be required, although such evidence may be presented as part of a case.

Consequently, answers B, C and D are incorrect.

Question 14

Answer **B** — Section 28 of the Road Traffic Regulation Act 1984 has been amended by the Transport Act 2000. There are no longer restrictions as to the time of day that an offence may be committed (formerly the hours were 0800 hrs to 1730 hrs). Answer A is therefore incorrect.

A further effect of the 2000 Act was that school crossing patrols are no longer restricted to stopping vehicles for *children* to cross. They may stop vehicles to allow anyone to cross safely. Answer C is therefore incorrect.

The offence may be committed by a person who is driving or propelling a *vehicle*. There is no requirement for a person to be driving a motor vehicle. Answer D is therefore incorrect.

9   CONSTRUCTION AND USE

STUDY PREPARATION

The area of construction and use probably typifies what most police officers associate with road traffic legislation.

Seen by many as pedantic 'train spotter' law dealing with minor mechanical issues, construction and use legislation is in reality of some practical significance to patrol officers and the wider remit of road safety.

The level of detail that police officers and examination candidates are expected to know has been greatly reduced over recent years but there is still quite a lot of factual information to absorb.

Although you could probably fill a book such as this with construction and use questions, you will be relieved to find that only a selection of some more relevant points has been included in this chapter.

QUESTIONS

Question 1

Regulation 27 of the Road Vehicles (Construction and Use) Regulations 1986 sets out the requirement for the depth of tread required for tyres fitted to motor vehicles, which are used on the road.

What is the minimum depth of tread allowed on such tyres?

[A] 1.6 mm throughout a continuous band across the whole of the tyre, and around the entire circumference.

[B] 1 mm throughout a continuous band across the central 3/4 section of the tyre, and around the entire circumference.

[C] 1 mm throughout a continuous band across the whole of the tyre, and around the entire circumference.

[D] 1.6 mm throughout a continuous band across the central 3/4 section of the tyre, and around the entire circumference.

Question 2

WATSON is a taxi driver. One evening, WATSON pulled up outside a customer's house and sounded the taxi's horn several times, to attract the person's attention. The customer lived in a built up area and WATSON's taxi was stationary. The time was 11.35 pm.

Has WATSON committed an offence under reg. 99 of the Road Vehicles (Construction and Use) Regulations 1986?

[A] Yes, because it was after 11.00 pm and the vehicle was stationary.

[B] No, because it was not before 11.30 pm.

[C] Yes, because the vehicle was stationary.

[D] No, because the vehicle was stationary.

Question 3

WINSTON parked outside a newsagent shop in his car. He was accompanied by BREEN, who was sitting in the front passenger seat. Before WINSTON entered the shop, he turned off the car engine, but forgot to set the handbrake. BREEN realised what had happened and pulled the handbrake up before WINSTON returned.

Has WINSTON committed the offence of 'quitting' in these circumstances?

[A]   Yes, provided BREEN was not a full licence holder.
[B]   No, as the engine was not left running.
[C]   No, as BREEN was in a position to intervene.
[D]   Yes, regardless of whether BREEN had a full licence.

Question 4

Section 40A of the Road Traffic Act 1988 deals with the use of a vehicle on a road, in a dangerous condition.

To which of the following does the term 'dangerous' apply?

[A]   Motor vehicle only, together with the passengers carried in or on it, or its accessories and equipment.
[B]   Motor vehicle or trailer, together with the passengers carried in or on it, or its accessories and equipment.
[C]   Motor vehicle, together with the passengers carried in or on it, or trailer together with its accessories and equipment.
[D]   Motor vehicle only, together with any accessories and equipment it is fitted with.

Question 5

DOMINGUEZ was driving his car on a road through a built up area at 1.00 pm, when he was stopped by Constable HIND. The officer examined DOMINGUEZ's car and discovered that the rear nearside light was defective.

What general exemption, under the Road Vehicles Lighting Regulations 1989, may DOMINGUEZ claim, to avoid prosecution for the defective light?

[A] None, as the exemption applies to headlamps only.
[B] That the defect occurred during the journey, or arrangements have been made to rectify it as soon as possible.
[C] That the defect occurred during the journey.
[D] That the defect has only recently occurred, and arrangements have been made to rectify it.

Question 6

Which of the following statements, if either, is/are correct, in relation to the testing of vehicles under s. 47 of the Road Traffic Act, 1988?

1. All motor vehicles must be tested three years after they were first manufactured.
2. All emergency vehicles must submit to a test after one year, instead of three.

[A] Statement 1 only.
[B] Statement 2 only.
[C] Both statements.
[D] Neither statement.

Question 7

CRAIG realised that the test certificate on his car had expired. His friend, WALSH, owned a garage and was authorised to issue MOT certificates. CRAIG drove his car to WALSH's garage, where it failed the MOT test. CRAIG made arrangements to return the car the next day for work to be carried out, in order to pass the test.

Has CRAIG committed an offence in relation to the vehicle in these circumstances, either by driving it to or from the garage?

[A] Yes, on his way there only, as he had not arranged a test for the vehicle in advance.
[B] Yes, on his way there and on his way home, as he had not arranged to test the vehicle in advance.
[C] No, as he was taking the vehicle to be tested, and returning it after it had been refused a certificate.
[D] Yes, on his way there only; he is exempt in relation to the return journey, as the vehicle had been refused a test certificate.

Question 8

Regulation 68 of the Road Vehicles (Construction and Use) Regulations 1986 provides police officers with the power to direct goods vehicles and large passenger carrying vehicles to a place to be examined.

What restrictions are placed on officers exercising these powers?

[A] Any such vehicle may be directed to any suitable place as directed by the officer.
[B] Stationary vehicles may be directed to a suitable place within two miles of the location.
[C] Stationary vehicles may be directed to a suitable place within five miles of the location.
[D] Any such vehicle may be directed to a suitable place within five miles of the location.

Question 9

Which of the following statements is/are correct in relation to the power under reg. 74 of the Road Vehicles (Construction and Use) Regulations 1986 to inspect vehicles on premises following a road traffic accident?

1. The power may be exercised police officers in uniform only.
2. There is no power of entry provided by the regulation.
3. The inspection must take place within 24 hours of the accident.

[A] Statement 1 and 2 only.
[B] Statement 2 only.
[C] Statements 2 and 3 only.
[D] Statements 1 and 3 only.

ANSWERS

Question 1

Answer **D** — Regulation 27 of the Road Vehicles (Construction and Use) Regulations 1986 (SI 1986 No. 1078) sets out a number of specific defects that will make tyres unlawful. The Road Vehicles (Construction and Use) (Amendment) (No. 4) Regulations 1990 (SI 1990 No. 1981) increased the depth of tread requirement to 1.6 mm from 1 mm. Answers B and C are incorrect for this reason.

The depth of tread must be 1.6 mm throughout a continuous band across the *central 3/4 section of the tyre*, and around the entire circumference. Answer A is therefore incorrect. Answer C is also incorrect for this reason.

Question 2

Answer **C** — Under reg. 99 of the Road Vehicles (Construction and Use) Regulations 1986, a person commits an offence by using the audible warning instrument while the vehicle is stationary on the road *or* if it is used between 11.30 pm and 7.00 am. The offence is complete if one of these circumstances is met. Answer B is therefore incorrect.

Answer A is incorrect as the offence is committed after 11.30 pm, not 11.00 pm.

Answer D is incorrect; the offence was committed because the vehicle *was* stationary.

Question 3

Answer **A** — Regulation 107 of the Road Vehicles (Construction and Use) Regulations 1986 prohibits motorists from leaving a motor vehicle unattended on a road unless the engine has been stopped *and* the handbrake has been set (*Butterworth* v *Shorthouse* [1956] Crim LR 341). This means that the offence will be committed if the driver allows either of these circumstances to occur. Answer B is therefore incorrect.

A driver will not commit an offence if the vehicle is left 'attended'. For a person to be 'attending' a vehicle in these circumstances he/she must be *licensed* to drive it *and* be in a position to intervene. Answers

C and D are incorrect; a person must be the holder of a full driving licence and be in a position to intervene.

Question 4

Answer **B** — Section 40A of the Road Traffic Act 1988 deals with *either* a motor vehicle or a trailer, which is used in such a way that involves a danger of injury to any person. Answers A and D are therefore incorrect.

The offence may be committed in a number of ways, including the number of passengers carried in or on either of the above vehicles, or the manner in which they are carried; *or* the condition of the vehicle itself or of its accessories and equipment. Answer C is therefore incorrect.

The offence may also be committed if the vehicle presents a danger because of the purpose for which it is used.

Question 5

Answer **B** — It is an offence under reg. 23 of the Road Vehicles Lighting Regulations 1989 (SI 1989 No. 1796) to use, cause or permit to be used a vehicle on a road unless the relevant lamps are clean and in good working order.

There is, however, an exemption under reg. 23(3): if the vehicle is being used during daytime hours and the defect only happened during the journey *or* if arrangements have been made to rectify it with all reasonable expedition. Answers C and D are therefore incorrect.

The exemption applies to all relevant lamps, not just headlamps. Answer A is therefore incorrect.

Question 6

Answer **D** — Both statements are incorrect.

All motor vehicles must be tested three years after they were first *used on the road*. Certain vehicles must be tested after one year from the time they were first used on the road. These include, motor vehicles having more than 8 seats, which are used to carry passengers, taxis, ambulances and large goods vehicles. Police vehicles and fire engines are *not* listed. In fact vehicles *provided* for police purposes are exempt from requiring a test certificate.

Consequently, answers A, B and C are incorrect.

Question 7

Answer **B** — There are exemptions to s. 47 of the Road Traffic Act 1988 (using a motor vehicle on a road without a test certificate), where a person is taking a vehicle to or from a testing station. However, a driver may only claim exemption if they are driving to *or from* a pre-arranged test. The key is whether the test was pre-arranged and in this case it was not. Answer C is therefore incorrect.

Although they are worded differently, answers A and D are incorrect for the same reason. There is a further exemption for vehicles, which have been refused test certificates. However, this exemption only applies when the vehicle is being driven, *by prior arrangement*, or brought from the relevant place where the work is being carried out. This exemption allows garage proprietors, who are not registered to supply test certificates, to take vehicles to and from testing stations and again does not apply in these circumstances.

The last exemption, which again does not apply to the given facts, is where a vehicle is being towed to be broken up, following the refusal of a test certificate.

Question 8

Answer **C** — The power conferred by reg. 68 of the Road Vehicles (Construction and Use) Regulations 1986 applies to *stationary* vehicles only. Answers A and D are therefore incorrect.

The regulation authorises a constable in uniform to direct a stationary vehicle to suitable premises, provided the place is no more than *five miles* from the location where the direction was made. Answers A, B and D are all incorrect for this reason.

Question 9

Answer **B** — Statement 1 is incorrect. Although the power under reg. 74 of the Road Vehicles (Construction and Use) Regulations 1986 relates to 'reportable accidents', it may be exercised either by a police officer in uniform *or* by an authorised vehicle examiner.

Statement 2 is correct. There is no power of entry provided by this regulation.

Statement 3 is incorrect. The inspection must take place within 48 hours of the reportable accident.

Consequently, answers A, C and D are incorrect.

10   TRAFFIC SIGNS

STUDY PREPARATION

What can you say about traffic signs? There are mercifully few key principles and powers to learn here . . .

QUESTIONS

Question 1

A religious festival was taking place over a two-day period in a large park. The police placed cones on the road outside the park, to prevent vehicles from parking outside and causing an obstruction. The officer in charge decided to leave the cones in place overnight, to restrict parking before the next day's event.

Did the officer in charge have the authority to leave the cones in place in between the two events?

[A] Yes, the officer may leave the cones in place for up to seven days from the time they were placed.
[B] No, the officer should have removed the cones following the potential obstruction and re-sited them before the next one.
[C] Yes, the officer may leave the cones in place for up to 36 hours from the time they were placed.
[D] No, the officer should have sought permission from the local traffic authority to maintain the cones in place following the original obstruction.

Question 2

In relation to the placing of a traffic triangle as a warning of a temporary obstruction, which of the following statements is correct?

[A] It must be used in conjunction with at least three other traffic triangles.
[B] It may be used in conjunction with a warning lamp.
[C] It must be used in conjunction with a warning lamp.
[D] It must be used in conjunction with three traffic cones.

Question 3

Which of the following statements, if either, is/are correct in relation to the power to direct traffic under s. 35 of the Road Traffic Act 1988?

1. The power is restricted to a mechanically propelled vehicle.
2. The power is not restricted to a police officer in uniform.

[A] Statement 1 only.
[B] Statement 2 only.
[C] Both statements.
[D] Neither statement.

Question 4

BECKER is a traffic warden who one day came across a road accident. BECKER began directing traffic until a police officer arrived. PETERS was walking along the pavement, which was blocked by one of the cars involved in the accident. BECKER asked PETERS to wait on the pavement until it was safe to walk in the road. PETERS refused to do so because he was in a hurry and walked out into the road, nearly causing another accident.

Did BECKER have the authority to demand PETERS' name and address in these circumstances?

[A] No, as this power is restricted to constables in uniform.
[B] No, as this power is restricted to constables.
[C] No, as a traffic warden's power is restricted to stopping vehicles.
[D] Yes, as PETERS failed to comply with the direction given to stop.

ANSWERS

Question 1

Answer **A** — A traffic sign will include 'any object or device (whether fixed or portable) for conveying to traffic on roads . . . warnings, information, restrictions or prohibitions of any description' (s. 64 of the Road Traffic Regulation Act 1984).

Traffic signs may be placed by a constable or other person authorised by the chief officer of police in order, amongst other things, to prevent congestion or obstruction from traffic. The signs may remain in place for up to *seven* days. Answers B and C are therefore incorrect.

There is no requirement to seek permission from the local traffic authority. Answer D is therefore incorrect.

Question 2

Answer **B** — Under reg.16 of the Traffic Signs (Temporary Obstructions) Regulations 1997 (SI 1997 No. 3053), traffic triangles must be placed at least 45 metres from the obstruction, facing approaching traffic.

There is no requirement for traffic triangles to be placed with any other similar triangles (answer A is therefore incorrect), or with other cones or signs (answer D is therefore incorrect).

A warning lamp may be used in conjunction with most traffic signs (including traffic triangles). However, this is not mandatory and therefore answer C is incorrect.

Question 3

Answer **B** — Statement 1 is incorrect; the power to direct vehicles under s. 35 of the Road Traffic Act 1988 is *not* restricted to mechanically propelled vehicles, it applies to *any* vehicle.

Statement 2 is correct, the power is *not* restricted to police officers in uniform, it applies to *any* police officer, as well as traffic wardens.

Consequently, answers A, C and D are incorrect.

Question 4

Answer **D** — A police officer in uniform engaged in the regulation of vehicular traffic in a road has the authority to stop pedestrians from proceeding (s. 37 of the Road Traffic Act 1988). This power is also given to traffic wardens (s. 96 of the 1988 Act). Answer C is therefore incorrect.

Under s. 169 of the Act, if a person fails to comply with a direction given under s. 37, a *constable* (not necessarily in uniform), has the authority to demand their name and address. Again, by virtue of s. 96 of the Act, this power is also given to traffic wardens. Answers A and B are therefore incorrect.

11 DRIVING LICENCES

STUDY PREPARATION

The law relating to driving licensing is of considerable practical significance.

You need to know how the licensing system works in terms of what licence is needed by what driver for what vehicle; you also need to know the relevant police powers in relation to licences and the attendant offences that can be committed.

Of particular importance is the offence of disqualified driving and the provisions that apply to learner drivers and their supervisors.

QUESTIONS

Question 1

Section 87 of the Road Traffic Act 1988 makes it an offence for a person to drive a motor vehicle on a road otherwise than in accordance with a licence.

In relation to the burden of proof that the defendant was driving on a road and that he or she had a licence to do so, which of the following statements is correct?

[A] The defence must prove that the defendant was not driving on a road, and that he or she had a licence to drive the vehicle.

[B] The prosecution must show that the defendant was driving on a road; the defendant must show that he or she had a licence to do so.

[C] This is an absolute offence; no further proof is required, other than the fact that the defendant was driving on a road.

[D] The prosecution must show that the defendant was driving on a road and that he or she had did not have a licence to do so.

Question 2

Section 164 of the Road Traffic Act 1988 provides a constable with the authority to demand the production of a driving licence from a person supervising the holder of a provisional driving licence.

Under what circumstances may a constable demand the production of a driving licence when such a person is no longer supervising a person who is driving a motor vehicle on a road?

[A] When he or she has reasonable cause to believe that the supervisor was committing an offence, or that the driver had been involved in an accident.

[B] Only when he or she has reasonable cause to believe that the driver was committing an offence.

[C] When he or she has reasonable cause to believe that the driver was committing an offence, or had been involved in an accident.

[D] When he or she has reasonable cause to believe that the person was supervising a driver who was driving a motor vehicle on a road.

Question 3

Constable HERSI was on duty, when she stopped BELL, a learner driver, who was driving a motor vehicle on a road. BELL was accompanied by MARTIN, who was supervising him. Constable HERSI asked BELL and MARTIN to produce their driving licences. However, only MARTIN had his with him.

From whom could Constable HERSI require a date of birth in these circumstances?

[A] Either, but only if she suspects BELL has committed an offence.
[B] Either, but only if she suspects that MARTIN is under 18.
[C] From BELL, as MARTIN has produced a driving licence.
[D] From either, but only if she suspects that MARTIN is under 21.

Question 4

Section 101 of the Road Traffic Act 1988 sets out the minimum ages to enable a person to drive certain classes of vehicles.

In relation to this section, which of the following statements, if either, is/are correct?

1. A person must be at least 18 years of age in order to drive a medium-sized goods vehicle.
2. A person must be at least 16 years of age in order to drive a moped.

[A] Statement 1 only.
[B] Statement 2 only.
[C] Both statements.
[D] Neither statement.

Question 5

KLINE was driving a motor vehicle on a road, when he was stopped by Constable POPE. KLINE admitted that he was only 16 and did not possess a licence to drive the vehicle.

What power would Constable POPE have to arrest KLINE in these circumstances?

[A]   None, KLINE should be reported for summons for driving other than in accordance with a licence.
[B]   KLINE can be arrested for driving whilst disqualified in these circumstances.
[C]   None, KLINE should be reported for summons for driving whilst disqualified.
[D]   KLINE can be arrested for driving whilst disqualified by reason of his age.

Question 6

In relation to the proof required to prove an offence of driving while disqualified under s. 103 of the Road Traffic Act 1988, which of the following statements is correct?

[A]   The prosecution will need to show the defendant was disqualified, and that he or she was aware of this fact.
[B]   The prosecution will need to show the defendant was disqualified, but not that he or she was aware of this fact.
[C]   The defendant will need to show that he or she was not disqualified, or that he or she was not aware of this fact.
[D]   The offence is one of strict liability; the prosecution need only show that the defendant was driving a motor vehicle on a road.

Question 7

JELF was driving a motor vehicle on a road, when she was stopped by Constable STACEY. JELF admitted that she had been recently convicted of speeding, and had been disqualified from driving until she passed a driving test. JELF was in possession of a provisional driving licence, but she was unaccompanied at the time she was stopped, and was not displaying 'L' plates.

What offence has JELF committed, and what power does Constable STACEY have to deal with her?

[A]   Disqualified driving; report JELF for summons only.
[B]   Failing to display 'L' plates and driving unaccompanied; report JELF for summons only.
[C]   Driving other than in accordance with a licence; report JELF for summons only.
[D]   Disqualified driving; JELF may be arrested.

Question 8

Which of the following statements, if either, is/are correct in relation to compulsory basic training courses for provisional licence holders riding motor cycles and mopeds?

1.   When a person completes a compulsory basic training course, he or she is issued with a certificate, which is valid for two years.
2.   An instructor taking a training course for motor cycles and mopeds may not supervise more than two provisional licence holders at one time.

[A]   Statement 1 only.
[B]   Statement 2 only.
[C]   Both statements.
[D]   Neither statement.

Question 9

POTTER was supervising GREEN, who was learning to drive. As they were travelling along the road, GREEN collided with a parked car. GREEN panicked and drove off after the accident, without stopping.

Does POTTER have a responsibility for GREEN's actions in these circumstances?

[A] Yes, but only if he encouraged the actions.
[B] No, he is only there to supervise GREEN's driving.
[C] No, he is only there to provide tuition for GREEN.
[D] Yes, he should have ensured that GREEN remained at the scene.

Question 10

ARNOLD was acting as a supervisor to MAHMOOD, who was driving a motor vehicle on a road. ARNOLD had given MAHMOOD several lessons, but was not a registered driving instructor. MAHMOOD did not pay ARNOLD directly for the lessons, but gave him money each time to cover the cost of petrol.

Does ARNOLD need to be registered to give driving lessons in these circumstances?

[A] No, as he was not being paid directly for the lessons.
[B] No, as he did not have a commercial arrangement with MAH-MOOD.
[C] Yes, as he had a commercial arrangement with MAHMOOD.
[D] No, any person may give driving lessons, if they have a full licence.

Question 11

Regulation 18 of the Motor Vehicles (Driving Licences) Regulations 1999 deals with new residents in the United Kingdom who hold a valid driving licence in their country of origin.

What do the Regulations state about the ability of such people to drive in the UK?

[A]   They may drive for 12 months, but must obtain a provisional driving licence before driving on a road.

[B]   They may drive for 12 months and may apply for a provisional driving licence during that time.

[C]   They may not use their foreign driving licence, as they are a resident not a visitor.

[D]   They may drive for 18 months and may apply for a provisional driving licence during that time.

Question 12

AMIR was involved in a road accident during the hours of darkness. A witness stated that AMIR had caused the accident by failing to comply with a 'Give Way' sign. AMIR admitted to Constable WARE that he normally wore contact lenses, but had forgotten to wear them that night.

Under what conditions may Constable WARE require AMIR to submit to an eyesight test?

[A]   In daylight conditions, while wearing his contact lenses.
[B]   In darkness, without his contact lenses.
[C]   In darkness, while wearing his contact lenses.
[D]   In daylight conditions, without his contact lenses.

ANSWERS

Question 1

Answer **B** — In proving the offence under s. 87 of the Road Traffic Act 1988, it is for the *prosecution* to show that the defendant was driving on a road. Answer A is therefore incorrect.

It is for the defendant to show that he or she had a licence to drive that class of vehicle (*John* v *Humphries* [1955] 1 All ER 793). In spite of this, it would be prudent for the prosecution to gather such evidence as is available to them, such as DVLA records.

Answer D is therefore incorrect.

Answer C is incorrect, for the above reasons.

Question 2

Answer **C** — Under s. 164 of the Road Traffic Act 1988, the power to demand production of a driving licence by a driver, or a person supervising the driver, of a motor vehicle on a road is restricted to the present tense only, where the driver is *not* suspected of *having committed an offence*, or *having been involved in an accident*. Therefore, if the officer simply has reasonable to cause to suspect a person *has been* driving a motor vehicle on a road, this would not provide sufficient authority to demand the production of a driving licence from either the supervisor or the driver. Answer D is therefore incorrect.

In order to demand production from a person who has been driving, the constable must have reasonable cause to believe that the *driver*, (answer A is incorrect, as it refers to the supervisor), was either committing an offence *at that time, or had been* involved in an accident. Answer B is incorrect, as the constable may do so in either of these circumstances.

Question 3

Answer **D** — The power to demand a person's date of birth in these circumstances is given by s. 164(2) of the Road Traffic Act 1988. If a person is driving a vehicle, and fails to produce a driving licence as requested, the officer may ask for his or her date of birth. There is no requirement to suspect that an offence has been committed. Answer A is therefore incorrect.

A constable may also demand a date of birth from a person, who is supervising a driver, if he or she suspects that person to be under 21 years of age. Answer B is therefore incorrect. This power would also apply even if the person has produced a driving licence, provided the constable had reason to suspect that he or she is under 21. Answer C is therefore incorrect.

Question 4

Answer **C** — A person will be disqualified from holding or obtaining a licence to drive a motor vehicle of a class specified in s. 101 of the Road Traffic Act 1988, if he or she is under the age specified for that class of vehicle.

Statement 1 is correct; the specified age for a medium-sized goods vehicle is 18. Statement 2 is also correct; the specified age for a moped is 16. Consequently, answers A, B and D are incorrect.

Question 5

Answer **A** — Even though a person who drives a certain class of vehicle under age will be 'disqualified' from holding a licence, that person will not commit an offence of disqualified driving under s. 103 of the Road Traffic Act 1988. They will commit an offence of driving other than accordance with a licence, under s. 87(1) of the Act. Answers B, C and D are all incorrect for this reason.

The power of arrest for disqualified driving will also not apply in these circumstances; therefore answers B and D are incorrect.

Question 6

Answer **B** — The offence under s. 103 of the Road Traffic Act 1988 is one of strict liability. However, the prosecution will need to show more than just the fact that the defendant was driving a motor vehicle on a road. Answer D is therefore incorrect.

The prosecution *will* need to prove that the defendant was, in fact, a disqualified driver. As the onus is on the prosecution, answer C is incorrect.

However, there is no need for the prosecution to prove that the defendant knew of the disqualification (*Taylor* v *Kenyon* [1952] 2 All ER 726). Answer A is therefore incorrect.

Question 7

Answer **D** — Where a person has been disqualified by the court until a test is passed, he or she has to comply with the requirements of a provisional licence holder. If a person fails to comply with these requirements, he or she commits the offence of disqualified driving (*Scott* v *Jelf* [1974] RTR 256). Answers B and C are therefore incorrect.

Where the person has committed the offence of disqualified driving, he or she may be arrested by a constable who has reasonable cause to suspect him or her of committing the offence. The power will apply in these circumstances. Answer A is therefore incorrect.

Question 8

Answer **A** — Statement 1 is correct. When a person completes a compulsory basic training course, he or she is issued with a certificate, which is valid for *two* years.

Statement 2 is incorrect. An instructor taking a training course for motor cycles and mopeds (compulsory basic training), may not supervise more than *three* provisional licence holders at one time. This is in contrast to an instructor taking a training course for 'large motor cycles' (direct access course). Here, the amount of students an instructor can safely train is two.

Consequently, answers B, C and D are incorrect.

Question 9

Answer **D** — A person supervising a learner driver is required not to provide tuition for the learner, but to 'supervise'. Answer C is therefore incorrect.

Supervising requires some positive action on behalf of the supervisor, and these duties extend to ensuring compliance with other legislative requirements, such as remaining at the scene of an accident (*Bentley* v *Mullen* [1986] RTR 7). Answer B is therefore incorrect. There is no need to show encouragement to commit the offence, merely that the supervisor did not act to prevent the actions. Answer A is therefore incorrect.

Question 10

Answer **C** — Any person may give driving lessons provided they do not charge money *or money's worth* in return. If a person wants to give driving lessons for payment, he or she must be registered in accordance with the provisions of Part V of the Road Traffic Act 1988. Answers A and D are therefore incorrect.

In the case of *Mahmood* v *Vehicle Inspectorate* (1998) 18 WRTLB 1, it was held by the Divisional Court that what mattered was that the instructor had some sort of arrangement with the learner driver and that the arrangement had a 'commercial flavour'. The fact that Arnold was receiving money's worth (a payment for petrol) may amount to a 'commercial flavour' for the purposes of this legislation. Answer B is therefore incorrect.

Question 11

Answer **B** — Under reg. 18 of the Motor Vehicles (Driving Licences) Regulations 1999, visitors *and* new residents holding a valid driving licence from their country of origin may use that licence as a full licence to drive on the roads. Answer C is therefore incorrect.

Such drivers may drive for up to 12 months using their licence, and they may take a test during that period. Answer D is therefore incorrect. Drivers *may* apply for a provisional licence during the period, but this is not compulsory. Answer A is therefore incorrect.

Question 12

Answer **D** — Regulations 72–73 of the Motor Vehicles (Driving Licences) Regulations 1999 (SI 1999 No. 2864) require a driver to be able to read a registration mark fixed to a motor vehicle from 20.5 metres. A constable may require a person to submit to an eyesight test if he or she has reason to suspect that the person was driving a motor vehicle on a road with defective eyesight.

The driver must be given the eyesight test in *good light*, whilst wearing corrective lenses if worn at the time. This means that if the person was *not* wearing corrective lenses, they must take the test *without* them. Answers A and C are therefore incorrect. Even if the offence took place in darkness, the driver must take the test in good light. Answers B and C are incorrect for this reason.

12 EXCISE AND REGISTRATION

STUDY PREPARATION

This is another highly practical area. Recent amendments to the legislation have increased the ways in which people seeking to avoid paying the relevant duty on vehicles can be brought to book.

In addition to these, you need to know the circumstances in which certain vehicles have to display some form of vehicle excise licence; you also need to know which vehicles require registration marks and who will be liable to a criminal penalty if they fail to do so.

QUESTIONS

Question 1

Certain vehicles are exempt from having to pay duty under the Vehicle Excise and Registration Act 1994.

In relation to the exemption, which of the following statements is correct?

[A] Vehicles over 25 years may be exempt, and they may be required to display a 'nil' licence.

[B] All vehicles over 25 years are exempt, however, they must display a 'nil' licence.

[C] Vehicles over 25 years may be exempt, however, they must display a 'nil' licence.

[D] All vehicles over 25 years are exempt, and they may be required to display a 'nil' licence.

Question 2

Which of the following statements, if either, is/are correct in relation to a vehicle, which is unlicensed under s. 29 of the Vehicle Excise and Registration Act 1994, being kept on a road?

1. Proceedings may only be brought under the section with the approval of the Secretary of State.
2. A person committing an offence under the section may be required to pay up to five times the annual duty rate, as well as any back duty owed.

[A] Statement 1 only.
[B] Statement 2 only.
[C] Both statements.
[D] Neither statement.

Question 3

Constable PLATT was on patrol with an officer from the DVLA, searching for unlicensed vehicles, with the intention of clamping them. They received a complaint of an abandoned vehicle, which had been obstructing a driveway for some weeks. The vehicle was not displaying an excise licence, and Constable PLATT arranged for it to be moved around the corner, where it was clamped.

Has Constable PLATT acted in accordance with powers given by the Vehicle Excise Duty (Immobilisation, Removal and Disposal of Vehicles) Regulations 1997 in these circumstances?

[A] No, the vehicle should not have been moved, it should have been clamped where it was found.
[B] No, the vehicle should not have been clamped, as it was an abandoned vehicle.
[C] Yes, the vehicle may be moved to a new location, where it may be clamped.
[D] No, the vehicle should not have been clamped; it was not displaying an excise licence which had expired.

Question 4

Section 33(1) of the Vehicle Excise and Registration Act 1994 makes it an offence to fail to display a licence when a vehicle is on a road.

Would the prosecution need to prove anything in relation to the defendant's state of mind, when prosecuting this offence?

[A] Yes, that the defendant was aware of the offence.
[B] No, the *defendant* must show he or she had no intent..
[C] No, it is for the *defendant* to introduce the statutory defence.
[D] No, the offence is one of absolute liability.

Question 5

HUMPHRIES owns a car showroom. However, his premises are not large enough to keep all the cars inside. During the daytime, HUMPHRIES parks many of his cars on the road outside. None of the vehicles is taxed and they are returned to the showroom at night. HUMPHRIES has six trade licences and places these on the vehicles when they are parked on the road.

Is HUMPHRIES entitled to keep the vehicles on the road while displaying trade licences in this manner?

[A]   Yes, provided he has a trade licence for each vehicle.
[B]   No, he may not keep the vehicles on the road in these circumstances.
[C]   Yes, provided they are on the road in the course of business.
[D]   Yes, if the vehicles are temporarily in his possession.

Question 6

Constable PENG saw an unattended vehicle parked on a road, not displaying an excise licence. Constable PENG made enquiries to establish the owner's identity, but was unable to do so. Two months later, Constable PENG stopped BOULD driving the vehicle. BOULD stated that he had bought the vehicle from a car dealer recently and was not the owner of it at the time of the offence. The vehicle was now displaying an excise licence.

Is Constable PENG entitled to ask BOULD for details of the previous keeper in these circumstances?

[A]   No, as BOULD was not the keeper of the vehicle at time of the offence.
[B]   Yes, but BOULD may have a defence if he is unable to provide the details.
[C]   Yes, and BOULD would have no defence if he is unable to provide the details.
[D]   No, Constable PENG may only make the enquiry with the dealer who sold the car.

Question 7

Who, if either, of the people below would commit an offence under the Road Vehicles (Display of Registration Marks) Regulations 2001 if their vehicle was used on a road?

1. PETERS has a motor vehicle, which was registered on 1 February 2001. The vehicle is fitted with registration plates whose characters are in italic script.
2. LEE owns a motor cycle, which was registered on 1 October 2001. LEE has fixed a number plate to the front and rear of the motor cycle.

[A] PETERS only.
[B] LEE only.
[C] Both.
[D] Neither.

Question 8

KANE owns a garage, which specialises as a body shop for spray painting cars. He instructed one of his workers, HEGG, to park a car on the road while they were awaiting a delivery. The car was not displaying registration plates, as they had been removed for the bodywork to be sprayed. HEGG parked the car outside the premises, and returned it about 20 minutes later.

Who, if anyone, would be guilty of an offence under s. 42(1) of the Vehicle Excise and Registration Act 1994 (failing to display a registration mark) in these circumstances?

[A] KANE only, as the keeper of the vehicle.
[B] HEGG only, as the driver of the vehicle.
[C] Both people, KANE as the keeper and HEGG as the driver.
[D] Neither person, as the vehicle was only temporarily on the road.

ANSWERS

Question 1

Answer **A** — Vehicles over 25 years *may* be exempt from having to pay excise duty, provided they were constructed *before* 1 January 1973.

Exempt vehicles *may* be required to display a 'nil' licence when used on a road.

Answer A is the only correct combination; therefore, answers B, C and D are incorrect.

Question 2

Answer **C** — Statement 1 is correct: proceedings may only be brought under s. 29 of the Vehicle Excise and Registration Act 1994 with the authority of the Secretary of State. The Secretary of State may provide authority for the police to bring proceedings by issuing a certificate of approval to do so (s. 47(4)).

Statement 2 is also correct; a person committing an offence under s. 29 may be required to pay up to five times the annual duty rate. He or she must also pay back the duty unpaid.

Consequently, answers A, B and D are incorrect.

Question 3

Answer **B** — The Vehicle Excise Duty (Immobilisation, Removal and Disposal of Vehicles) Regulations 1997 (SI 1997 No. 2439), empower 'authorised persons', such as the police and the DVLA, to clamp certain vehicles when the authorised person has reason to believe that an offence has been committed under s. 29 of the Vehicle Excise and Registration Act 1994, in relation to that vehicle. The fact that the vehicle is not displaying a licence would give rise to such suspicion and therefore, answer D is incorrect.

The vehicle may either be clamped where it is, or moved to another location and clamped. Answer A is therefore incorrect.

Certain vehicles are exempt from being clamped and abandoned vehicles are included in this list (presumably because there is little prospect of recovering duty from such a vehicle). The vehicle in question *should not* have been dealt with using this power. Therefore, answer B is correct, which means that answer C is incorrect.

Question 4

Answer **D** — The offence is one of absolute liability and the prosecution have no duty to prove a guilty state of mind, even if the licence was removed by another person (*Strowger* v *John* [1974] RTR 124). Answer A is therefore incorrect.

There is no statutory defence, and because the offence is one of absolute liability, there is no provision for the defendant to establish a defence. Answers B and C are therefore incorrect.

Question 5

Answer **B** — Under s. 34(1)(c) of the Vehicle Excise and Registration Act 1994, a person may not use a trade licence to keep a vehicle on a road unless it is done so in circumstances under s. 12(1)(c) of the Act (carrying goods/passengers for testing). The fact that he has trade licences for all the vehicles would not allow Humphries to park vehicles on the road for these purposes. Answer A is therefore incorrect.

Trade licences may be used only in the course of a person's business, however, not in these circumstances. Answer C is therefore incorrect.

Lastly, trade licences may be used only on vehicles which are temporarily in a trader's possession, but again, not in these circumstances. Answer D is therefore incorrect.

Question 6

Answer **B** — The *current keeper* of a vehicle is obliged to provide details of the keeper of the vehicle at the time of the offence, even if that person was not the keeper at that time (s. 46(1)(a) of the Vehicle Excise and Registration Act 1994 and see *Hateley* v *Greenough* [1962] Crim LR 329). Answer A is therefore incorrect.

Section 46(2)(b) of the 1994 Act requires *any other person* to provide such information as is in his power to give as to the identity of the person who kept the vehicle on a road at the time of the offence. This would include asking the car dealer in the scenario, but because of the above, is not restricted to that person. Answer D is therefore incorrect.

There is a statutory defence provided by s. 46(6), if a person charged with an offence is able to satisfy the court that he or she did not know, and could not with reasonable diligence have ascertained, the identity of the person or persons concerned. Answer C is therefore incorrect.

Question 7

Answer **B** — The circumstances in statement 1 do not amount to an offence under the Road Vehicles (Display of Registration Marks) Regulations 2001. It will be an offence for a vehicle first registered *on or after* 1 September 2001 to be fitted with registration plates whose characters are in italic script. Vehicles registered before this date are not affected (reg. 15).

The circumstances in statement 2 *do* amount to an offence under the above Regulations. Any motor cycle first registered *on or after* 1 September 2001 *must not* be fitted with a registration plate to the front. Vehicles registered before this date *need not* be fitted with such plates (reg. 6).

Consequently, answers A, C and D are incorrect.

Question 8

Answer **C** — Under s. 42 of the Vehicle Excise and Registration Act 1994, the 'relevant person' commits an offence, if he or she 'drives' a vehicle on a road, when it is not displaying a registration mark. HEGG would commit the offence; therefore answers A and D are incorrect.

Where the vehicle is not being driven, the 'keeper' will commit an offence under this section. A person will be the 'keeper' if he or she causes the vehicle to be on a public road for any period, *however short*, when it is not in use. Therefore, as KANE was responsible for causing the vehicle to be on the road, he also commits the offence. It is irrelevant how long the vehicle was on the road. Answers B and D are therefore incorrect.

13 GOODS AND PASSENGER VEHICLES

STUDY PREPARATION

In common with several other areas, the law relating to goods and passenger vehicles has been condensed in the *Blackstone's Police Manuals*. Nevertheless, there is still a lot of detail, particularly in terms of the different categories of vehicle (seating, weight etc.).

Operators' licences, drivers' hours and power of enforcement are all key areas of this topic. So too are the laws regulating the licensing and use of taxis.

QUESTIONS

Question 1

In relation to the definitions of goods vehicles and passenger carrying vehicles, which of the following statements, if any, is/are correct?

1. A large goods vehicle (LGV) is a motor vehicle used for carrying goods, having a maximum permissible weight over 7 tonnes.
2. A large passenger carrying vehicle (PCV) is one which is used for carrying more than 16 passengers.
3. A small passenger carrying vehicle (PCV) is one which is used for carrying more than 12 passengers, but fewer than 16.

[A] Statements 1 and 2 only.
[B] All of the above.
[C] Statements 2 and 3 only.
[D] Statement 2 only.

Question 2

Regulation 16(8) of the Motor Vehicles (Driving Licences) Regulations 1999 prohibits holders of provisional driving licences from carrying passengers in certain circumstances, when they are driving a passenger carrying vehicle.

In relation to those restrictions, which of the following statements is correct?

[A] They apply only when a person is undergoing a driving test.
[B] They apply only to large passenger carrying vehicles.
[C] They apply only to drivers under 21.
[D] They apply only when a person is not undergoing a driving test.

Question 3

MORRIS is 20 years of age, and the holder of a provisional LGV driving licence. MORRIS has appeared in court for an offence of speeding, which takes the number of penalty points on his driving licence to six.

What does reg. 56 of the Motor Vehicles (Driving Licences) Regulations 1999 say in relation to MORRIS being disqualified from holding a LGV licence?

[**A**] He must be disqualified if he accumulates 12 penalty points.

[**B**] He must be disqualified now.

[**C**] He may be disqualified now.

[**D**] He must be disqualified if he accumulates *more than* 6 penalty points.

Question 4

PARKER wishes to hire a small passenger carrying vehicle (PCV) to take his friends to a football match. The cost of the vehicle is to be shared amongst the friends. PARKER does not have a PSV licence.

In which circumstances may PARKER drive such a vehicle?

[**A**] He must be over 18 and have held an ordinary driving licence for at least two years.

[**B**] He must be over 21 and have held an ordinary driving licence for at least two years.

[**C**] He must be over 21 and have held an ordinary driving licence for at least 12 months.

[**D**] He may not drive such a vehicle, as he is not the holder of a full PSV licence.

Question 5

ALBERT owns a bakery company, which produces its own cakes and bread. All goods produced at the bakery are delivered using 15 vans, which are owned by ALBERT. Each of the vans has a 'plated' weight of 5 tonnes.

Does ALBERT require an operator's licence in these circumstances?

[A] No, the vehicles are too small.
[B] Yes, a standard operator's licence.
[C] Yes, a restricted operator's licence.
[D] No, the vehicles are not used for hire or reward.

Question 6

BASHIR owns the Travel Lodge Hotel, situated near an airport. BASHIR has purchased a small mini bus designed to carry 12 passengers. He intends to offer guests the facility of a ride to the airport from his hotel. Guests will not be charged extra for the facility; however, BASHIR has included the journey in the cost of the room.

Does BASHIR's vehicle qualify as a public service vehicle (PSV) in these circumstances?

[A] Yes, it is a PSV and BASHIR will need an operator's licence.
[B] No, as passengers are not required to pay separate fares.
[C] Yes, it is a PSV, but BASHIR will not require an operator's licence.
[D] No, because the vehicle is not being used for hire or reward.

Question 7

Which of the statements below, if either, is/are true in relation to public service vehicles and passenger carrying vehicles?

1. Under the Public Service Vehicles (Conduct of Drivers, Inspectors, Conductors and Passengers) Regulations 1990, a constable may demand from a person who has contravened the Regulations his or her name and address.
2. The driver of a community bus must hold a PSV licence, as well as a community bus permit, in order to drive on the road.

[A] Statement 1 only.
[B] Statement 2 only.
[C] Both statements.
[D] Neither statement.

Question 8

Part VI of the Transport Act 1968 regulates drivers' hours for certain types of vehicles.

Which of the following vehicles are generally covered by the Act?

[A] Passenger carrying vehicles constructed or adapted to carry more than 8 passengers.
[B] Passenger carrying vehicles constructed or adapted to carry more than 16 passengers.
[C] Passenger carrying vehicles constructed or adapted to carry more than 12 passengers.
[D] All public service vehicles, regardless of how many passengers are carried.

Question 9

What are the daily and weekly driving hours that are generally acceptable in order to comply with Part VI of the Transport Act 1968?

[A] Ten hours daily driving, with no more than 56 hours per week.
[B] Eight hours daily driving, with no more than 50 hours per week.
[C] Nine hours daily driving, with no more than 56 hours per week.
[D] Nine hours daily driving, with no more than 40 hours per week.

Question 10

In relation to the issue and retention of tachograph record sheets, which of the following statements is correct?

[A] It is the driver's responsibility to ensure that he or she has enough tachographs; drivers must also ensure that they are kept for at least one year.

[B] Employers must ensure that sufficient tachographs are issued to each driver, and employers must ensure that they are kept for at least one year.

[C] It is the driver's responsibility to ensure that he or she has enough tachographs; employers must ensure that they are kept for at least one year.

[D] Employers must ensure that sufficient tachographs are issued to each driver, and employers must ensure that they are kept for at least two years.

Question 11

In relation to the production and submission of tachograph record sheets, which of the following statements is correct?

[A] Employers must be able to produce drivers' sheets for the current week; drivers must return completed sheets to their employer within 21 days.

[B] Drivers must be able to produce sheets for the current month; they must also return completed sheets to their employer within 21 days.

[C] Drivers must be able to produce record sheets for the current week; they must also return completed sheets to their employer within 28 days.

[D] Drivers must be able to produce record sheets for the current week; they must also return completed sheets to their employer within 21 days.

Question 12

Constable UNDERHILL is dealing with a road traffic accident, involving a heavy goods vehicle which drove off without stopping. Constable UNDERHILL visited CLEGG, whose company owns the vehicle. The company is based in the UK. Constable UNDERHILL requested from CLEGG the tachograph record sheet relating to the vehicle on the day of the accident.

What power would be available to Constable UNDERHILL if CLEGG refused to produce the required document?

He could:

[A]   Stop the vehicle being driven on a road until the required document is produced.
[B]   Stop the vehicle being driven on a road and direct it to be removed to a police station until the document is produced.
[C]   Report CLEGG for obstruction and stop the vehicle being driven on the road until the document is produced.
[D]   Detain the vehicle in question until the document is produced.

Question 13

Which body (outside the Metropolitan and London police areas) has the responsibility for providing a licensing system for hackney carriages to ply for hire as taxis?

[A]   The local authority.
[B]   The magistrates' court.
[C]   The police.
[D]   The Secretary of State.

Question 14

WILLIS has bought a vehicle, which she intends to use as a hackney carriage. WILLIS intends to ply for taxi fares in two neighbouring districts in the South West of England. One area is a busy shopping centre, where she would work in the daytime; the other area is located near a number of night clubs, where she would work in the evening. However, the two districts are controlled by separate licensing bodies.

How many licences should WILLIS apply for, in order to work in the two districts?

[A] WILLIS may hold only one licence and she may only work in one district.
[B] WILLIS requires two licences, one for each district.
[C] WILLIS may hold only one licence, but each district she works in will be named on the licence.
[D] WILLIS may hold only one licence, but there are no restrictions on where she works.

Question 15

In relation to the regulations governing the issue of licences to taxi drivers, which of the following statements, if either, is/are correct?

1. Where an authority has decided to refuse a licence to an applicant, they must believe beyond reasonable doubt that he or she is not a fit and proper person.
2. If a vehicle is licensed as a hackney carriage in one district, it can also be licensed as a private hire vehicle in another district.

[A] Statement 1 only.
[B] Statement 2 only.
[C] Both statements.
[D] Neither statement.

Question 16

STIRLING has recently had his hackney carriage licence revoked when it was due for renewal, as he was not a fit and proper person. STIRLING lived next door to a public house, where many of the customers had used his services in the past. One busy Saturday night, STIRLING sat in his taxi on his driveway, which was in full view of the public house, at closing time, hoping that when people came out, they would approach him asking for a taxi ride home.

Has STIRLING committed an offence of plying for hire without a licence in these circumstances?

[A] Yes, but only if he is approached by a customer.
[B] No, he would need to make some positive move towards the people.
[C] Yes, the offence is complete in these circumstances alone.
[D] No, he is not plying for hire on a road or in a public place.

Question 1

Answer **D** — Statement 1 is incorrect; a large goods vehicle (LGV), is a motor vehicle used for carrying goods, having a maximum permissible weight over 7.5 tonnes.

Statement 2 is correct; a large passenger carrying vehicle (PCV), is one which is used for carrying more than 16 passengers.

Statement 3 is incorrect; a small passenger carrying vehicle (PCV), is one which is used for carrying more than 8 passengers, but fewer than 16.

Consequently, answers A, B and C are incorrect.

Question 2

Answer **D** — Under the Motor Vehicles (Driving Licences) Regulations 1999 (SI 1999 No. 2864) the holder of a passenger carrying vehicle provisional driving licence must not carry passengers other than a supervising qualified driver or a full licence holder who is giving/receiving instruction. These restrictions *do not* apply during a driving test. Answer A is therefore incorrect.

The restrictions apply to the use of any passenger carrying vehicles by provisional driving licence holders, not just large PCVs. Answer B is therefore incorrect. They also apply to any provisional licence holder and not just persons under 21. Answer C is therefore incorrect.

Question 3

Answer **B** — Under reg. 56 of the Motor Vehicles (Driving Licences) Regulations 1999, if the holder of a LGV licence is under 21 years of age and he or she accumulates more than *three* penalty points (or is disqualified), that person *must* be disqualified from holding a LGV licence. Answers A, C and D are incorrect for this reason.

Question 4

Answer **B** — A person who is not the holder of a PSV licence may drive a small PCV without a full PSV licence for social purposes, other than for hire or reward and on behalf of a non-commercial body (reg. 7 of the Motor Vehicles (Driving Licences) Regulations 1999). Since the hirer of the van meets these requirements, answer D is incorrect.

Further conditions are imposed on a driver of a small PCV in the above circumstances. The person must be over 21 years of age, and have held an ordinary driving licence for at least *two* years. Answers A and C are therefore incorrect.

Question 5

Answer **C** — There are two types of operator's licences — 'standard' and 'restricted'. A restricted licence will be required for a person who is using vehicles in connection with his or her trade or business *other than the carriage of goods for hire or reward*. Since the person in the scenario is carrying his *own* goods, he requires a restricted licence. Answers B and D are therefore incorrect.

An operator's licence is *not* required if the vehicles being used are small goods vehicles, which are vehicles with a plated weight of 3.5 tonnes or less. The vehicles in the scenario are 5 tonnes; therefore an operator's licence is required. Answer A is therefore incorrect.

Question 6

Answer **A** — Under s. 1 of the Public Passenger Vehicles Act 1981, a public service vehicle (PSV) is:

(1)   a motor vehicle (other than a tramcar) which—
  (a)   being a vehicle adapted to carry more than eight passengers, is used for carrying passengers for hire or reward; or
  (b)   being a vehicle not so adapted, is used for carrying passengers for hire or reward at separate fares in the course of a business of carrying passengers.

The vehicle in the scenario is designed to carry more than eight passengers, therefore to qualify as a PSV you would have to prove that passengers were being carried for hire or reward (under s. 1(1)(a) above). Hotel courtesy buses have been held to be PSVs on the basis that the service was part of the overall hotel 'service', the cost of which was included in the price of a room or meal (*Rout* v *Swallow Hotels Ltd* [1993] RTR 80). This mirrors the scenario given and therefore answer D is incorrect.

There is no need to prove that the vehicle was being used for carrying passengers at separate fares (under s. 1(1)(b)), as the vehicle is designed to carry more than eight passengers and qualifies as a PSV under s. 1(1)(a). Answer B is therefore incorrect. All PSVs being used on a road for hire or reward require an operator's licence, irrespective of the type of service provided (s. 12). Answer C is therefore incorrect.

Question 7

Answer **D** — Statement 1 is incorrect; where a person commits an offence under the Public Service Vehicles (Conduct of Drivers, Inspectors, Conductors and Passengers) Regulations 1990 (SI 1990 No. 1020), the power is given to the driver, conductor or inspector of a PSV to demand that person's name and address. The power is not given to a constable.

Statement 2 is incorrect; the driver of a community bus *may* hold a community bus permit which *exempts* him or her from the need for a PSV licence.

Consequently, answers A, B and C are incorrect.

Question 8

Answer **C** — Part VI of the Transport Act 1968 generally applies to PSVs and other motor vehicles constructed or adapted to carry more than 12 passengers. Answers A and B are therefore incorrect.

There are exemptions for vehicles that are not required to carry passengers for long distances, normally those controlled by public authorities. Not all PSV drivers are restricted by the rules; therefore answer D is incorrect.

Question 9

Answer **C** — Under Part VI of the Transport Act 1968, the acceptable hours are, normally nine hours daily driving period, but ten hours no more than twice a week. The total period of driving for any one week must not exceed 56 hours, (or 90 hours per fortnight). Answers A, B and D are therefore incorrect.

Question 10

Answer **B** — It is the employer's duty to ensure that all drivers working for them have sufficient tachographs. The drivers have the responsibility to ensure that the tachos are in use when they drive the vehicles. Answers A and C are therefore incorrect.

Employers must also ensure that tachograph sheets are retained for at least *one* year, for inspection on request of an authorised inspector. Answers A and D are incorrect for this reason.

Question 11

Answer **D** — Under the Community Recording Equipment Regulations, *drivers* must be able to produce tachograph record sheets for the current *week* (and also for the last day of the previous week they drove). Answers A and B are therefore incorrect.

Drivers must also return completed sheets to their employer within *21* days. Answer C is incorrect for this reason.

Question 12

Answer **D** — Under s. 99(1) of the Transport Act 1968, a constable (or authorised person), may require any person to produce and permit him or her to examine and copy any record sheet that that person is required to retain or be able to produce. For the purpose of exercising the power, the constable/authorised person may detain the vehicle during such time as is required for the exercise of the power.

If the *driver* of a vehicle obstructs a constable or fails to comply with a requirement made, the constable (or authorised person), may prohibit the person from driving the vehicle on a road. The constable/authorised person may also direct the vehicle to a place specified by him or her. Since the constable in the question was dealing with the owner and not the driver, this second power is not applicable and answer A is therefore incorrect.

An officer exercising the power above could direct the vehicle to any place, not just a police station. However, again this power applies when dealing with the driver of a vehicle and therefore answer B is incorrect.

A person failing to comply with any requirement to allow inspection of records would commit a specific offence under s. 99 of the 1968 Act and therefore could be reported for that offence and not obstruction. Answer C is therefore incorrect.

Question 13

Answer **A** — Under s. 37 of the Town Police Clauses Act 1847, local authorities have the responsibility for providing a licensing system for hackney carriages to ply for hire as taxis. Answers B, C and D are therefore incorrect.

Note. In London the system for hackney carriages and private hire vehicles is provided under the Metropolitan Public Carriage Act 1869. The licensing authority is Transport for London.

Question 14

Answer **B** — Under the Local Government (Miscellaneous Provisions) Act 1976, all hackney carriage licences are issued by a particular district. Therefore, in order to ply for hire in more than one district, a hackney carriage driver would have to apply for one licence for each district. There appears to be no limit on the number of licences a person may apply for. Answers A, C and D are incorrect for this reason.

Question 15

Answer **B** — Statement 1 is incorrect; if an authority refuses a person's hackney carriage licence, the decision may be based on the civil law standard of proof — 'balance of probabilities' (see *R* v *Maidstone Crown Court, ex parte Olson, The Times*, 21 May 1992).

Statement 2 is correct; a vehicle licensed as a hackney carriage in one district may be licensed as a private hire vehicle in another district (*Kingston-upon-Hull Council* v *Wilson, The Times*, 25 July 1995).

Question 16

Answer **C** — It is a summary offence to operate, drive or ply for hire without the relevant licence. The Divisional Court held that 'plying for hire' can extend to a situation where the vehicle is in a prominent position on private property just off a street when the public was there in numbers (*Eastbourne Borough Council* v *Stirling and Morley, The Times*, 16 November 2000). Answer D is therefore incorrect.

A taxi driver may be 'plying for hire' by simply being parked in a prominent position. There is no requirement to prove that the defendant made some positive move towards the public, or even that he or she was actually approached by a customer. Answers A and B are therefore incorrect.

14 FIXED PENALTY SYSTEM

STUDY PREPARATION

The Fixed Penalty Notice system is pretty straightforward. Understand the principles behind it and you will realise that the system is simply designed to speed up the administration of some common offences which won't result in disqualification.

The flowcharts in the *Blackstone's Road Traffic Manual* are useful in seeing the whole system at work.

QUESTIONS

Question 1

RICHIE was stopped by Constable WELLER for a speeding offence. Constable WELLER intended issuing RICHIE with a fixed penalty notice for the offence. RICHIE did not have his driving licence with him, but stated that there were some points on it, although he could not remember how many.

Under what circumstances could RICHIE be made to surrender his driving licence for the offence, if he produces it within seven days?

[A] None, as he did not have it with him at the time, he should be reported for the offence.

[B] He must produce it to a constable or authorised person, provided he is not likely to exceed 11 points for this offence.

[C] He must produce it to a constable in uniform, provided he is not likely to exceed 12 points for this offence.

[D] He must produce it to a constable or authorised person, provided he is not likely to exceed 12 points for this offence.

Question 2

Which of the following statements, if either, is/are correct in relation to the fixed penalty procedure under the Road Traffic Offenders Act 1988?

1. A fixed penalty may not be issued, where the offence is one of causing or permitting an offence specified in the schedule.

2. Where the offence committed does not involve an obligatory endorsement, a fixed penalty may only be issued in relation to a stationary vehicle.

[A] Statement 1 only.

[B] Statement 2 only.

[C] Both statements.

[D] Neither statement.

Question 3

Section 75(8)(1)(a) of the Road Traffic Offenders Act 1988, specifies a period, during which a person issued with a conditional offer of a fixed penalty, may make a payment in order to avoid attending court.

What is the length of the specified period?

[A]   14 days.
[B]   21 days.
[C]   One month.
[D]   28 days.

Question 4

Which of the following statements, if either, is/are correct in relation to the issue of fixed penalty notices under the Road Traffic Offenders Act 1988?

1. A traffic warden has the same powers as a constable to issue fixed penalty notices, but only in relation to non-endorsable notices.
2. If a person has submitted his or her driving licence with a conditional fixed penalty notice and they are liable for disqualification, the licence will be returned to the police.

[A]   Statement 1 only.
[B]   Statement 2 only.
[C]   Both statements.
[D]   Neither statement.

ANSWERS

Question 1

Answer **B** — A person may be issued with a fixed penalty notice, (FPN), if he or she commits an offence to which the procedure applies (in this case, an endorsable offence). The person may not be issued with a FPN if he or she would be liable for disqualification if convicted for the offence. A person would be disqualified under the 'totting up' procedure if their driving licence shows *12 points* or more. Answer D is incorrect as a FPN may be issued only if the points are likely to *exceed* 11 points, not 12.

If a person does not have his or her licence at the time of the offence, he or she may be required to produce it within seven days and therefore answer A is incorrect. There is a safeguard built in here because if it is discovered at this stage that the penalty points are likely to reach 12 points, the driving licence will not be surrendered.

Finally, the driving licence may be produced either to a constable in uniform *or* an authorised person, such as an enquiry clerk at a police station. Answer C is therefore incorrect.

Question 2

Answer **C** — Statement 1 is correct; s. 51(2) of the Road Traffic Offenders Act 1988 specifies that a person may be issued only with a fixed penalty notice if the offence relates to the 'use' of the vehicle on a road. The system does not apply to those who 'cause' or 'permit' the use of a vehicle on a road while an offence is being committed.

Statement 2 is also correct; s. 62(1) of the Road Traffic Offenders Act 1988 allows a constable to affix a notice to a *stationary* vehicle. The purpose of s. 62(1) is to enable a non-endorsable FPN to be issued where the driver is not present. Presumably the legislators envisaged practical problems with attempting to affix such a notice to a moving vehicle!

Consequently, answers A, B and D are incorrect.

Question 3

Answer **D** — Under s. 75(8)(a) of the Road Traffic Offenders Act 1988, the specified period is 28 days and therefore answers A, B and C are incorrect.

Question 4

Answer **D** — Statement 1 is incorrect. Under the Functions of Traffic Wardens (Amendment) Order 1986 (SI 1986/1328) a traffic warden has the same powers as a constable to issue fixed penalty notices, for *both* endorsable and non-endorsable offences.

Statement 2 is also incorrect; if a person is sent a conditional offer of a fixed penalty notice, and that person is liable for disqualification, the payment and the licence will be returned to the *defendant* and the police will be notified (s. 76(4) of the Road Traffic Offenders Act 1988). This would give the police the opportunity to proceed by way of summons.

Consequently, answers A, B and C are incorrect.

15 PEDAL CYCLES

STUDY PREPARATION

There's not *that* much you can — or can't — do with a bike. Therefore, there's not that much a trainer or examiner can do with a bike question . . .

QUESTIONS

Question 1

What is the minimum age at which a person may ride an electrically assisted pedal cycle on a road?

[A]   15 years.
[B]   16 years.
[C]   14 years.
[D]   17 years.

Question 2

What is the maximum speed at which an electrically assisted pedal cycle may be ridden on a road?

[A]   15 miles per hour.
[B]   20 miles per hour.
[C]   30 miles per hour.
[D]   25 miles per hour.

Question 3

How many braking systems must be fitted on a either a fixed wheel or a free wheel pedal cycle made on or after 1 August 1984?

[A]   On a fixed wheel cycle, two; on a free wheel cycle, one.
[B]   One or two systems on either cycle.
[C]   Two systems on both cycles.
[D]   On a fixed wheel cycle, one; on a free wheel cycle, two.

Question 4

OWEN had been drinking for most of the day in a pub situated in a pedestrian precinct and left in a drunken state. OWEN had his pedal cycle with him, but felt too drunk to ride it. He pushed it along the busy precinct, bumping into people as he went. Constable WEAVER was passing by and witnessed the behaviour.

What action may Constable WEAVER take in respect of OWEN under the Road Traffic Act 1988?

[A] None, as OWEN is not on a road.
[B] Arrest OWEN for being in charge of a cycle whilst drunk.
[C] Report OWEN for being in charge of a cycle whilst drunk.
[D] None, as OWEN is not riding the cycle.

Question 5

Section 31 of the Road Traffic Act 1988 places a requirement for cycle races on public ways to be authorised before they take place.

Of the people listed below, who may commit an offence in relation to a cycle race which is not authorised?

[A] A person advertising the race, promoting or taking part in it.
[B] A person promoting the race or taking part in it.
[C] A person promoting the race, taking part in it or spectating.
[D] A person promoting the race only.

ANSWERS

Question 1

Answer **C** — Under s. 32 of the Road Traffic Act 1988, the minimum age at which a person may ride an electrically assisted pedal cycle on a road is 14 years and therefore answers A, B and D are incorrect.

Question 2

Answer **A** — Under the Pedal Cycles (Construction and Use) Regulations 1983 the maximum speed at which an electrically assisted pedal cycle may be ridden on a road is 15 miles per hour and therefore answers B, C and D are incorrect.

Question 3

Answer **D** — Under the Pedal Cycles (Construction and Use) Regulations 1983 (SI 1983 No. 1176), a pedal cycle made on or after 1 August 1984 must comply with the following:

- On a free wheel cycle, two independent braking systems: one acts on the front wheel and one on the rear.
- On a fixed wheel cycle, one braking system acting on the front wheel.

Answer D is the only correct combination and therefore answers A, B and C are incorrect.

Question 4

Answer **D** — A person commits an offence under s. 30 of the Road Traffic Act 1988, if they *ride* a cycle on a road or public place when unfit to ride it through drink or drugs. There is no mention of being 'in charge' for an offence under this section. Answers B and C are therefore both incorrect.

Had the person been riding the cycle, he would have committed an offence, as the offence may occur in a public place. Answer A is therefore incorrect. Further, there is no power of arrest for an offence under the section. Answer B would still have been incorrect.

An offence may also be committed in these circumstances under s. 12 of the Licensing Act 1872 (but *not* under the Road Traffic Act 1988), of being in charge of a carriage in a public place while drunk.

Question 5

Answer **B** — The offence under s. 31 of the Road Traffic Act 1988 is committed by either the person promoting the race or taking part in it, when the race or speed trial was not authorised. Answers A, C and D are therefore incorrect.

16 FORGERY AND FALSIFICATION

STUDY PREPARATION

The end of the road — or at least road traffic.

There are relatively few offences involving forgery and falsification though, as much road traffic law — and its enforcement — relies upon records, these offences are more relevant than they may at first appear.

QUESTIONS

Question 1

UNION was stopped while driving PIPER's car on a road and was asked to produce his driving documents. UNION did not have his own policy of insurance. PIPER did not have insurance either, as he had failed to keep up his monthly payments and his insurance company had cancelled the policy. PIPER was still in possession of the insurance certificate, and he lent this to UNION for him to produce it. UNION was aware of the situation when he produced the documents.

Have either UNION or PIPER committed the offence of forgery of documents under s. 173 of the Road Traffic Act 1988?

[A] Yes, UNION only commits this offence in these circumstances.
[B] Yes, UNION and PIPER both commit this offence in these circumstances.
[C] Yes, PIPER only commits this offence in these circumstances.
[D] Yes, UNION commits this offence; PIPER is guilty of aiding and abetting.

Question 2

Section 174 of the Road Traffic Act 1988, deals with the offence of making false statements and withholding information.

What would the prosecution need to show in order to prove an offence under this section?

[A] The offence is one of specific intent, and the prosecution must show that the defendant gained from the transaction.
[B] There is no need for the prosecution to prove intent, or that the defendant gained from the transaction.
[C] The offence is one of specific intent, but there is no need to show the defendant gained from the transaction.
[D] There is no need to prove intent, but the prosecution must show the defendant gained from the transaction.

Question 3

Constable GRAY stopped SEWELL driving a car on a road. SEWELL produced a set of documents to Constable GRAY; however, the officer suspected that the test certificate had been altered. Constable GRAY seized the document and SEWELL admitted knowing that it was forged.

In relation to the test certificate, what action may Constable GRAY take under s. 176 of the Road Traffic Act 1988?

[A] Arrest SEWELL for the offence of altering the document.
[B] Summons SEWELL to appear in court to account for his possession of the document.
[C] Report SEWELL for the offence of altering the document.
[D] Report SEWELL for the offence of altering the document and summons him to appear in court to account for his possession of it.

ANSWERS

Question 1

Answer **B** — Under s. 173(1)(b) of the Road Traffic Act 1988, a person commits an offence if, with intent to deceive, he or she lends to, or allows to be used by any other person, a document or other thing to which the section applies. Certificates of insurance are covered, and where a person produced a certificate of insurance issued under a policy, which had expired, the offence is made out (*R v Cleghorn* [1938] 3 All ER 398). Therefore, Piper is guilty of the full offence, by lending/allowing Union to use the insurance certificate.

Under s. 173(1)(a) of the Road Traffic Act 1988 a person who, with intent to deceive, is guilty of an offence if he or she 'uses' a document to which this section applies. Union is guilty of 'using' the document when he produces it. Answers A, C and D are therefore incorrect.

Question 2

Answer **C** — The offence under s. 174 of the Road Traffic Act 1988 is one of specific intent; therefore answers B and D are incorrect.

There is no need to show that the person actually gained anything or brought about the desired consequences (see *Jones v Meatyard* [1939] 1 All ER 140). Answers A and D are incorrect for this reason.

Question 3

Answer **C** — There is no power of arrest for an offence contrary to s. 176 of the Road Traffic Act 1988, therefore answer A is incorrect.

Section 176(2) allows for a person to be summonsed before a magistrates' court to account for his or her possession of a document seized under s. 176(1). However, this power may be exercised only when the document has been returned to him or her, or when he or she has not been summonsed or charged for an offence connected with the document. Given Sewell's admission, it is likely that he will be prosecuted for the offence, and it is not necessary to summons him separately using the power under s. 176(2). Answers B and D are therefore incorrect.